THE PALACES
OF PRAGUE

THE PALACES
OF PRAGUE

Photographs by
Lubomir Pořizka

Text by
Zdeněk Hojda and Jiří Pešek

TAURIS
PARKE
BOOKS

Published in 1995 by
Tauris Parke Books
An imprint of I.B.Tauris & Co Ltd
45 Bloomsbury Square
London WC1A 2HY

Copyright © 1994 Blanckenstein Verlag, Munich
Design and layout: Lucchetti-Bergame
Endpapers: Prague in 1600
Translated from German by Francisca Garvie

A full CIP record of this book is available from
the British Library

ISBN 1 86064 005 2

Printed and bound in Italy

Contents

Historical background 7

1. Prague Castle:
   The Old and New Royal Palace 22
2. The House of the Lords of Kunstatt . . 34
3. The Royal Summer Palace or Belvedere . 36
4. Schwarzenberg Palace 42
5. Hrzán Palace 46
6. Martinicz Palace 50
7. Waldstein Palace 54
8. Michna Palace 60
9. Lobkovicz Palace (Hradčany) 64
10. Nostitz Palace 68
11. Czernin Palace 72
12. Kolowrat-Novohradsky Palace 80
13. Troja Palace 84
14. Toscana Palace 94
15. Liechtenstein Palace 98
16. Kaiserstein Palace 100
17. Sternberg Palace 102
18. Lobkovicz Palace 108
19. Morzin Palace 112
20. Clam-Gallas Palace 116

21. Schönborn Palace 122
22. Thun Palace 124
23. Kolowrat-Thun Palace 128
24. Villa Amerika 132
25. Kaunitz Palace 138
26. Mladota Palace (Faust House) 140
27. Grand Prior's Palace 142
28. Colloredo-Mansfeld Palace 150
29. Buquoy Palace 154
30. Sylva-Taroucca Palace 164
31. Fürstenberg Palace 170
32. Goltz-Kinsky Palace 174
33. Archbishop's Palace 180
34. Turba Palace 188
35. Pachta Palace 190
36. Kolowrat Palace 194
37. Thun Palace, the Bohemian Diet 200
38. Rohan Palace 204
39. Schebeck Palace 206
40. Villa Lanna 210
41. Villa Groebe 212
    Map 216

The Palaces of Prague

Historical background

The Czech poet Vítězslav Nezval (1900–58) described Prague as "an old town of portals, Baroque statues, and banks." And it is true that portals and statues go together in Prague, adorning the façades of churches, mansions, and, above all, palaces including banks, which are the palaces of the 19th and 20th centuries. The buildings of the aristocracy, the Church, and the bourgeoisie were constructed at much the same time, in much the same area, and in much the same kind of style, lining the streets of Prague in the form we see today.

The panorama of Prague Castle, with its Royal Palace and the silhouette of St. Vitus's Cathedral, is depicted in the first known view of Prague, a woodcut in the *Schedelsche Weltchronik* of 1493. Still the city's foremost emblem, Prague Castle has been the seat of kings and then presidents for eleven centuries. The tradition began at the end of the 9th century with the followers of Prince Borivoj (d. 894), the first historically documented Prince of the Premyslid dynasty, on a long ridge above the point where the Brusnice stream flows into the River Vltava, near a ford. Still earlier, there had been a sporadically settled fortress on the site, and it could be that the bulwarks above the rapids of the Vltava were once a place of heathen worship. From the time of Borivoj, however, the Premyslid princes made it their primary base, where a small church dedicated to the Virgin would soon be erected.

The first royal palace rose in the eastern part of what is now the third courtyard. According to archaeologists, it was a wooden structure on stone foundations supporting a ground floor and one story above. The palace must have stood here by the beginning of the 11th century, since an account of the investiture of Prince Bretislav in 1034 tells of coins being thrown down to the people from the upper story.

By the beginning of the 12th century the royal seat of the princes had come to be called a "palace," according to the *Chronicon Bohemorum* of Kosmas of Prague, Canon of the Prague Chapter, who related the history of Bohemia from its mythical beginnings up to his own times. That Kosmas used this term for the royal seat presumably reflects his knowledge of Classical models, but it is just as likely that he employed "palace" to distinguish between the royal residence and the splendid Romanesque strongholds of the nobility, built below the castle *(suburbium)* on major trade routes along the right bank of the Vltava.

In the second quarter of the 12th century, under Prince Sobeslav, a new four-story stone building was erected with a tower gate and its own chapel, the latter dedicated to All Saints in 1182. This ambitious residence, the ground floor of which is still well preserved below the Old Royal Palace, went on being used by the Premyslid princes and kings without any major structural alterations until the fire of 1303. Then, during a period marked by power struggles and weak rule, the palace was left to deteriorate for three decades. In 1333, when Margrave Charles, later King and then Emperor Charles IV, began governing the country in the name of his father, John of Luxembourg, he had at first to live in the town below. But the Royal Palace soon awoke to new life, once the stone masons from the workshop of Master Matthias of Arras began building an impressive Gothic residence on the ruins of the Romanesque structure, styling it to the taste of the Luxembourg Prince, who had been educated in the tradition of French country life. The scale of the new palace was to reflect the enhanced status of the sovereign, and

The first known view of Prague, a woodcut from the Schedelsche Weltchronik *of 1493.*

the importance of Prague as the spiritual center of the Holy Roman Empire.

By this time the royal residence already overlooked three towns. In the 1230s, the economically and politically dominant "Old Town" or "Greater Town" of Prague began to take shape on the right bank of the Vltava. Meanwhile, below the castle, on the left bank of the river, a new town, later called the "Lesser Town" of Prague, grew up on the site of an earlier settlement. Finally, in 1348, Emperor Charles IV improved the urban complex of Prague with a splendid new act, which produced the "New Town", a wide band surrounding the territory of the Old Town. The area of land encompassed by these three communities would be sufficient to accommodate the growth of Prague right up until the 19th century.

At the beginning of the 13th century, this trio of lively towns proved more convient than the castle "island", with the result that the last Premyslid, Wenceslas III, rented a comfortable mansion appropriate to his needs near the Dominican monastery in the Old Town. What this house looked like is unknown, but recent excavations indicate the original form of the palace of John of Luxembourg, Charles IV's father. King John had converted a house "At the Ball" on the Old Town Square, originally the

property of a certain Petzold, a goldsmith from Eger, into an impresive town residence. Recent restoration has disclosed a tall, three-story building with high narrow windows. Its façade was articulated with niches containing life-size statues, figures now identified as a seated royal couple flanked by two princes bearing arms. Sadly, only fragments of the statues had survived, which made it impossible to reinstall them.

It was late-medieval Prague that saw the erection of more princely palaces. The ground floor of the Romanesque house belonging to the Lords of Kunstadt in Retezová survives today, as does part of the ground of the Maravian Margraves's palace, commissioned in 1335 by John Henry, Charles IV's brother, on the site of the present Clam-Gallas Palace. At the time, before the construction of the dam on the Vltava to supply water for the mill wheels and waterworks, the ground level in this part of the Old Town was several meters lower than it is today. Once alluvial and other deposits raised the level of the Old Town's narrow streets, the Romanesque and Early Gothic ground floors became cellars, which is how they survived the passage of time.

Still, many of the palaces that embellished 14th-century Prague have not survived. The palace in Stupartská that John of Luxembourg renovated in

8

1335 in the "Gallic manner" for Queen Beatrice, his second wife, stood until the beginning of the 20th century, when it was finally demolished. About the same time as well, an Art Nouveau building, erected on the north side of the Old Town Square, swept away the last remnants of the palace of Margrace Jost, a nephew of Charles IV. The palace belonging to the Dukes of Troppau on the northern part of what is now Charles Square in the New Town caught fire in 1434 and subsequently disappeared. In the Lesser Town all the residence of the archbishop in 1344, is a hidden tower. Contemporary sources chararcterize the builiding as a place in " the French style" with a royal chapel, a sculpture gallery, and a series of idealized portraits of the bishops of Prague. The episcopal domicile and its library were razed at the beginning of the Hussite movement. Simultaneously, the nearby palace of the Saxon dukes and

Prague in 1750, engraved from a drawing by L. Rohbock.

I. Rohbock del.ᵗ   J Riegel sculp.ᵗ

electors, adjacent to the smaller of the two towers on the Lesser Town side of the Charles Bridge, suffered serious damage. Actually, this onetime ducal seat, which had a spacious hall on the first story above the ground floor and a façade adorned with sculptures, no longer belonged to the Saxon dynasty, for in 1407 the grandson of Duke Rudolph I of the Saxony-Wittenberg, who had received the property from Charles IV, sold it to the Old Town. Later the Saxon palace would be rehabilitated in the Renaissance style, and today the building makes a rather more modest impression than in its former days of glory.

It is interesting to note that the term "palace" gradually disappeared in the 14th century, after which it would be reserved for the royal residence in the castle. Until the 17th century, the owners of town palaces had to content themselves with the term "house" or "mansion", regardless of the dwelling's size or architecture. It was not until the Baroque period that the aristocracy began once again to use the term "palace" (*palác*), or the French *palais,* for their town houses, at the same time that they described their rural seats as "châteaux" (*zámek*).

Charles IV, Bohemian King and Holy Roman Emperor, moved the royal residence back to Prague Castle. Taking the Louvre in Paris as his model, the monarch ordered a spacious palace built, complete with a banqueting hall on the first upper story, a grandiose room embellished with a portrait gallery of the Emperors who had preceded him. Although the castle buildings, at the center of which stood the Gothic cathedral erected by Peter Parler on the site of Romanesque churches, fully reflected the status of the Imperial occupant, they did not persuade Charles's successors to remain there. Even his son, Wenceslas IV, a cultivated lover of art if not a very

The Malostranské námešti in 1840.

successful politician, moved his court in 1383 to a palace – the Royal Court – on the eastern edge of the Old Town, a site now occupied by the Municipal House. The core of the academic quarter came into being here when Wenceslas gave the university the patrician palace of the mint-master Rotlev. This became the Carolinum, even today the heart of Charles University and one of the oldest scholastic buildings in the world. During the 15th century other Bohemian Kings would take up residence in the Royal Court.

Only in the reign of Vladislav II, from the Jagellon dynasty of Poland, did court life return to the castle palace, for a brief duration after the young King, startled by the Prague uprising of 1483, opted for the safer heights of the fortified royal enclosure. Crowned King of Hungary in 1492, Vladislav then moved permanently to Ofen in Budapest.

The first, hesitant steps towards a Renaissance style in Prague, taken during the reconstruction of the Royal Palace, did not bring about a revival of palatial architecture. Nothing encouraged the erection of such buildings, given that Ferdinand I of Habsburg preferred Vienna, despite both the Turkish threat and the promise made by the monarch, before his election to the throne of Bohemia in 1527, that he would settle in Prague. The Old Royal Palace in Prague Castle remained a ceremonial building, an architectural shell used for special occasions and meetings of the Diet and the Law Court. And yet Ferdinand liked Prague, as witnessed by the buildings he created in an attempt to escape the impasse of his confrontation with the Bohemian Estates and engage in more private activities. The Emperor had Italians plant orchards

Waldstein Palace in an 1840 engraving by Johann Poppel.

11

and ornamental gardens beyond the northern castle moat, where he also introduced a breath of Mediterranean air into the raw climate of Bohemia. By 1540 the ground floor of what became known as the Belvedere was habitable.

A major opportunity to rebuild Prague came when a raging fire broke out in the Lesser Town "Bastei" house and spread until it demolished a large part of Hradčany, which had sprung up to the west of the castle, and it severely damaged a substantial part of the castle itself. The left bank of the Vltava now underwent major reconstruction, which would include splendid aristocratic seats erected on the sites of incinerated houses. Even the exterior of the royal residence would be updated in the new Renaissance style.

Renovation of the castle began immediately, and by 1546 the Royal Palace had been rebuilt, its gables now decorated with sgraffito. However, the main impetus for new construction came in the wake of what is known as the Schmalkalden War (1546–47). Ferdinands son, Archduke Ferdinand of Tyrol, who was married to the lovely Philippine Welser, arrived in Prague to serve as Governor. A dilettante architect, Archduke Ferdinand drew up his own plans for the remarkable star-shaped Hvězda summer house on White Mountain and had them executed by Italian builders and stucco workers. He appointed Bonifaz Wohlmut royal architect and set about having the royal castle transformed in a manner that combined Gothic tradition with the efficiency and comforts introduced by the Renaissance. Moreover, Ferdinand encouraged renewed contacts with European cultural centers in Spain and Italy. Soon familiar with the Renaissance way of life abroad, dozens of young Bohemian aristocrats returned and re-created it at home. New stables were constructed next to the bridge leading into the Royal Gardens, not just for practical purposes but also to provide a social center for young nobles in need of a place to train their thoroughbred horses. Under Rudolph II the stables would become still more imposing. Meanwhile, the Ball Games Court, designed in the Palladian style, rose on the castle hill but did not reach completion until after 1567. By this time Archduke Ferdinand no longer lived in Prague, and Maximilian II had become King of Bohemia.

It was Archduke Ferdinand's son, Emperor Rudolph II, who chose Prague as his seat. However, the new monarch was in no hurry to move, and not until the court architects Hans Vredeman de Vries and Ulrico Aostalli had refurbished the royal residence did he appear in Prague to stay. Rudolph II had a new palace built above the southern ramparts of the castle, and the beautifully designed Paradise Gardens laid out below. The new Emperor lived in Prague from 1583 onwards, and the thirty or so years that followed his arrival are regarded by art historians as the Golden Age of Prague.

Under Rudolph II, Prague ceased to be the sleepy mother of the Bohemian towns, as it had been during the youth of Ferdinand I, and became a modern city with an important court, an archbishopric, and a new Jesuit University as well as a distinguished old university. Most of all, it had acquired a large number of new palaces. The townspeople being politically and economically too paralyzed to rebuild the burnt-out areas with any speed, the nobility leapt into the breach, for they now felt increasingly bound to Prague, not only by their more regular duties in the centralized administration of the kingdom, but also by the social

Waldstein Palace in an 1840 engraving by Johann Poppel.

allure of the court. The four most powerful families in Bohemia – the Lords of Rosenthal (Rožmitál), Schwanberg (Svamberk), Rosenberg (Rozmberk), and Pernstein (Pernštejn) – had their mansions erected right in the castle precincts, east of the Old Royal Palace.

The most luxurious edifice, constructed after 1573 by the architect Aostalli, was the palace of Wilhelm von Rosenberg, the most powerful nobleman in the kingdom and the pretender to the Polish throne. However, after the death of Wilhelm in 1590, the palace, with its luxurious interior and Italian garden on the south terrace, fell into neglect. The nearby Pernstein Palace, the last of the aristocratic residences in the castle's eastern precinct, was built in the 1570s for Vratislav von Pernstein,

13

Gen. u. l. Lange.　　　　　　　　　　　　Stahlst. v. Joh. Poppel

Czernín Palace in an 1840 engraving by Johann Poppel.

Lord Chancellor of the Kingdom of Bohemia, and decorated on the exterior with sgraffito and terracotta reliefs. Lord Vratislav did not live long to enjoy it, and after he died his daughter Polyxena conveyed the house as marriage dowry to her neighbor Wilhelm von Rosenberg and then to Zdenko Adalbert, her second husband and the first Prince von Lobkovicz, after whom the palace is still called.

The patrician palaces just outside the castle complex were as beautiful as those within, the most remarkable being the large residence of Jan von Lobkovicz, now known as the Schwarzenberg Palace, situated above the steep southern slope of Castle Square. This palace dominates the Hradčany panorama when viewed from the Lesser Town. Just below the Castle Steps stands what may very well be the most beautiful of the Renaissance palaces, a property originally owned by the Neuhaus family. It was this kind of mansion that many parvenus, such as Andres Teyfl von Kinsdorf, built in an attempt to gain entry into "high society." Andreas Teyfl spent so heavily to build his ambitious residence on the northwest corner of Castle Square that he found himself obliged to sell the place as soon as it had been completed to the Martinicz family.

By this time the palaces of Prague reflected their owners desire not only to impress but also to enjoy comfort. The interiors abounded in tapestries and carpets, objets d'art, goldsmiths' work, and, of course, paintings, especially portraits. Outside there were little balconies and roof terraces where the fortunate residents could admire the view, relax, and play music. Porticos, arcaded courtyards, and little gardens contributed towards an atmosphere of charm and intrigue. Despite the overwhelming influence of Italian Renaissance palaces, the realities of life in a northern climate yielded an architecture with a number of special features. But Italy also provided the model when Bohemian grandees began building country houses near Prague, the better to supply their urban kitchens more efficiently than would have been possible from greater distances. While scarcely any of these bucolic dwellings have survived, they are known from written sources, such as the records revealing much about the "summer house" of the Lords of Neuhaus in Butovice, now the fifth district of Prague. Here Adam von Neuhaus maintained a small palace with a surrounding park and a lovely view overlooking a swan-inhabited lake. Here again the design was inspired by royal precedent, for the King had one hunting lodge built in the deer park of Star Château (Hvežda) and another in the orchard.

The royal residence in the castle also underwent radical change, to such a degree that the original buildings erected by Rudolph II can no longer be seen, Classicized as they were in the 18th century during the reign of Empress Maria Theresia, Queen of Bohemia. Nevertheless, Rudolph II, more than any other ruler, except Charles IV, commissioned a variety of buildings in the castle complex. In the northwest precinct he had a new wing added with a gallery and the Spanish Hall, there installing the bulk of his remarkable art collections. On the other side of Stag Moat, along the edge of the beautifully tended Royal Gardens, the monarch erected the Lion's Court, connected to the palace by a long, roofed gallery through which he could reach the gardens unobserved.

The idyllic era of Rudolph II came to an abrupt end after the troops of Leopold von Passau invaded Prague in 1611 and plundered the palaces and houses of the Lesser Town. And this was merely a prelude to the Thirty Years' War, which exploded in 1618 after Protestant members of the Bohemian Estates threw the Emperor's Catholic Governors, Wilhelm of Slavata and Jaroslav of Martinicz, from a window in Prague Castle. Having survived their defenestration, by falling into a dung heap collected in the moat, the two Governors slid down the steep southern slope of the castle hill to an annex erected by King Ludvík (1510–26) next to the Old Palace, there to be hidden away by loyal servants from the nearby palace of Polyxena von Lobkovicz. The Bohemian uprising, the first act in a long war, brought executions, confiscations, and the emigration of more than a quarter of Prague's highly productive bourgeoisie. It also resulted in a change of ownership for many of the aristocratic residences. The Catholic Church, with its splendid processions, increasingly dominated urban life, just as the cityscape would be increasingly marked by the new façades and towers of Catholic monasteries and convents, colleges, churches, and chapels. The re-Catholicized University of Prague regained its former splendor, also, just as in the Middle Ages, a Chancellor in the person of the Archbishop of Prague, who resided a mere few steps from the Royal Palace in a Renaissance mansion hard by the western gate of the castle.

Still, the traditional bourgeois culture dating from before the Battle of the White Mountain (1620) continued in Prague until near the end of the Thirty Years' War, even as the ambitious new bureaucrats increasingly took the nobility as role models. Not all of the artists associated with the courtly Mannerism favored by Rudolph II left Prague when the royal court did, and some of these willingly offered their services to the new masters, among whom Count Albrecht von Waldstein (generally known in English as Wallenstein) figured very large indeed. The owner of a palace complex second only to Prague Castle, Waldstein would still be imitated, often by equally ambitious operators, more than twenty years after his fall from grace in 1634. The towns on the left bank of the Vltava, once plundered by the Swedish Army at the end of the Thirty Years' War, were so weakened and impoverished that initially they made no attempt to resist the construction of new aristocratic dwellings, which began to sprout on the combined sites of destroyed town houses, always free of tax and independent of the municipalities.

Maintaining a residence in Prague had now ceased to be a necessary evil and become a social and practical necessity. As a result, the new landed aristocracy acquired estates and offices, developed into real civil servants, and spent more and more of their time in town. The social and cultural climate of Prague satisfied even the most demanding of the nobles, with the result that Prague carried on court life despite the absence of princes of the blood. Not only did the city lie well away from the dangerously aggressive Turkish Army; it even served as a refuge for the Imperial court when, in 1679–80, Vienna fell prey to a raging epidemic of plague. Prague, moreover, became the seat of the four faculties restored to the University, and in 1717 it acquired the Bohemian Estates' School of Engineering. Also present were the archbishop and his court, together with many religious orders, all of whose scholastic, scientific, and cultural activities, magnificent liturgy and other ceremonies endowed the city with considerable glory.

The second half of the 17th century and the beginning of the 18th saw a major revival of patrician building in Prague. The same period also witnessed a resurgence of patriotic nationalism, but even while defending the last vestiges of their class and sovereign rights, the Bohemian nobility could still respond fully to the latest developments in European culture. Indeed, they returned home from their foreign tours and diplomatic travels totally captivated by the new things they had learned in Italy and France. Until the 1670s, the tendency was for Italian architects to bring their experiences and talents to Central Europe, a tradition begun in the Renaissance, and then adapt them to local conditions, working together with their Bohemian counterparts. At the turn of the 18th century, local Bohemian and sometimes Austrian architects as well produced key works on their own, works merely inspired by the Italian "founding fathers." In addition to secular buildings, the

A statue of Wenceslas (910-935),
the first Christian Prince of
the Přemyslid dynasty and
the patron saint of Bohemia.

ambitious aristocrats of Prague also commissioned architecture for religious foundations.

By this time Prague could boast some two hundred Baroque palaces, not all of which have, needless to say, survived in their original form. During the hasty construction of the New Town in the 19th century, what had been patrician gardens gave way to densely built-up areas. Further damage came with the reconstruction of the Old Town at the beginning of the 20th century. However, not all was lost, for luckily the aristocratic Lesser Town has remained largely intact.

During the Baroque period, the palaces of the Prague nobility did not so much adapt to their bourgeois environment as dominate it. Instead of country seats, the aristocracy now built urban palaces to reflect their status and serve as "showpieces." The interiors of these residences expressed the ambitions of a new elite, who opened their palaces to the "public," meaning members of the Bohemian Estates. The mansions also became the scene of various cultural activities, especially those with music rooms, since many of Prague's aristocrats were excellent musicians. The programs went so far as to include opera and theater performances. The nobility also counted many passionate collectors,

18

The crown jewels of Bohemia displayed in the St. Wencelas Chapel within the Cathedral of St. Vitas.

and their picture galleries, such as the Czernín Collection and the collection of Count Vrsovice, figured among Europe's most famous "curiosities." Needless to say, the grandiose urban seats of the Bohemian patriciate constituted more than residential palaces, embracing as they did servants' quarters, stables, riding schools, and gardens. In addition, the grandees of Prague surrounded the city with summer houses. Unfortunately, the cultural aims of this privileged class and their love of building did not always coincide with their financial resources, and the sheer extravagance of the Baroque era succeeded in bankrupting many a Bohemian aristocrat.

Prague as viewed by E. Thieme in 1834.

The interest of the Bohemian nobility turned towards Vienna only in the 18th century, after the Habsburg Empire reached the pinnacle of its power under Charles VI, followed by the centralization policies of his daughter, the Empress Maria Theresia. By the end of the Rococo century Prague had become a provincial backwater, the beginnings of which occurred with the military occupation of Prague by the French in 1741. The troops proved gallant enough in their behavior, and even gave the city a certain psychological lift, but their presence constituted a mere prelude to years of struggle for the Austrian inheritance, a struggle that would include two "visits" by the Prussian Army. Even so, Prague did see the erection of several new mansions during the Rococo period, among them the grand Kinsky Palace on the Old Town Square and the playful Sylva-Taroucca Palace next to the moat. Be that as it may, the spirit of the times is most clearly reflected in the uniformity of the reconstruction carried out in Prague Castle by Nicolo Pacassi. This royal architect buried variety under a uniformly Classical façade, spare in its artistic expression and plain as well as cool in its monumentality.

During the reign of Joseph II and the ensuing Napoleonic wars, the Bohemian nobility remained in the forefront of political and cultural developments. It was now that Prague knew a few more moments of glory, as at the 1787 premiere of Mozart's *Don Giovanni* in the private Nostitz Theater and the magnificent coronation ceremonies for Leopold II in 1791. Yet, the mentality of the times had changed quite notably, with pomp giving way to function and simplicity of form. The desire for luxury found expression only on the interior of buildings and in a search for comfort and intimacy. Beginning in 1815, aristocratic patrons of the arts found themselves in competition with the newly knighted bourgeoisie – financiers, businessmen, large landowners – who more and more had an impact on the taste of the times. Prague no longer knew the lively salon life of earlier days, nor did the Bohemian capital see the erection of ambitious new architecture. Quite simply, Prague "before the revolution" of 1918 assumed a provincial and sleepy air.

Soon after the 1866 war Prague gained permission to tear down its circuit of defensive walls. However, there was no way that the city could copy Vienna's Ringstrasse, given that the ramparts led through hilly terrain totally unconducive to a wide and imposing boulevard. Prague had to make do with the promenade along the moat and Ferdinand Street (now Národní), created after 1760 when the medieval fosse between the Old and New Towns was

filled in. The only new section was the short stretch over old ditches in the southeastern part of the New Town, where the municipal park was laid out in front of the former Franz Joseph Railway Station (now the Main Station). This area, between Wenceslas Square, the municipal park, and the moat, was the hub of commercial and social life for the German-speaking elite of Prague. It included a stock exchange, a German casino, and the New German Theater, opened in 1887. During the 1860s and 1870s the area also gained several modest Neo-Renaissance mansions, among them the Danek and Schebeck Palaces. A generation later the Czech bourgeoisie would also build in the New Town, splendid houses erected on the banks of the Vltava and styled in the Eclectic and Art Nouveau manners.

By the time Czechoslovakia became an independent state in 1918 the era of the great aristocratic mansions was truly over. The new palaces belonged to banks, savings institutions, corporations, and the agencies of the young Republic. Land reforms and the breach between Bohemia and the areas formerly under the monarchy subverted the wealth and social position of the old nobility, who found it difficult even to maintain their palatial residences. Increasingly the properties passed into the hands of the state and entered service as foreign embassies, schools, and ministries. The nationalizations that came after 1945 merely took the process to its ultimate, radical conclusion. Those palaces utilized in ways more or less consistent with their original purpose, such as the embassies, have survived in good condition, while others less fortunate have fallen into disrepair. It remains to be hoped that they will some day be suitably restored and once again allowed to play a determining role in the cityscape of Prague.

Prague Castle
The Old and New Royal Palaces

The Royal Palaces within the precinct of Prague Castle constitute the core of the agglomeration on the castle hill, and it is here that the Kings of Bohemia actually lived. Their symbolic seat, however, included the castle as a whole: the Cathedral of St. Vitus, the chapter houses, the Basilica of St. George, the palaces of the nobility, and a large number of public and residential buildings. In a still larger sense, not only the castle but also the adjacent community served as the royal seat, for whenever the King was in Prague, part of his court had to be accommodated below the castle in the town itself, which the royal presence inevitably coopted.

The Old Royal Palace

As the locus of the highest power in the Bohemian state, the Old Royal Palace forms a secular counterpart to St. Vitas's Cathedral. The cellars incorporate the remains of the 12th-century Romanesque palace of Sobeslav I, while the ground floor includes the rooms of the palace of Charles IV, who added a three-story chapel, styling it in the exquisite High Gothic manner of the Sainte Chapelle in Paris.

The Old Royal Palace assumed much of its present form during the reign of the Jagellons and the early Habsburgs. After the civil uprising of 1483,

which prompted King Vladislav to move from his Old Town palace to the greater security of Prague Castle, the monarch instigated much new building in the royal complex, work carried out under the direction of the architects Hans Spiess and Benedikt Ried, the latter taking over in 1489. This enterprise continued even after 1492, when King Vladislav moved his court to Ofen in Budapest. Since the Old Palace was meant to satisfy the requirements of a sovereign seat, it would always contain royal apartments, rooms situated on the piano nobile of the wing through which the palace is entered by way of the third courtyard. The royal chambers themselves led over a covered bridge into the Royal Oratory in St. Vitus's Cathedral. In this wing, the ground-floor room with the Late Gothic "net" vaulting, known as "Vladislav's bedchamber," served as the Chancellery of the Supreme Court, and it still lies behind the Green Room, where the Court formerly sat. As this suggests, the new building erected by King Vladislav did not function primarily as a royal residence, but rather a place of official and administrative functions performed at the highest level.

The magnificent Vladislav Hall, built where three halls once stood on the piano nobile of Charles

Vladislav Hall, built in the Old Royal Palace by Benedikt Ried. Tournaments were once held in this stupendous Flamboyant Gothic chamber. Participants entered the hall under the magnificent star vaulting of the Riders' Staircase.

IV's palace, forms the heart of the building. It is the largest medieval hall in Europe with stupendous fan vaulting held aloft without benefit of supporting piers; moreover, it is one of the most spectacular spaces ever constructed by human hands. Sixty-two meters long, 16 meters wide, and 13 meters high, Vladislav Hall is crowned by a monumental lierne vault of sinuous, gracefully intertwining ribs and illuminated by large Renaissance windows dating from 1493, which makes them one of the earliest manifestations of Renaissance architecture outside Italy. The hall was used for coronations, oaths of allegiance, and other court ceremonies, such as the reception of foreign ambassadors. For the jousting tournaments that also took place in Vladislav Hall, a special ramp was built – the Late Gothic Riders' Staircase fashioned of wide, flat wooden steps. Towards the end of the 16th century this breathtaking chamber also functioned as a kind of marketplace, where works of gold as well as rare fabrics, books, paintings, engravings, and so forth could be traded. The Prague elite, courtiers, and foreign visitors

Ignác Platzer's Battling Giants *frame the ceremonial entrance to the royal complex from the Castle Square.*

would congregate here to exchange information from every corner of the globe. As late as the 18th century, the great hall provided the setting for coronation banquets and magnificent balls. After 1918 it became the venue for formal sessions of the Czechoslavak Parliament, presidential elections, and major "state" exhibitions.

On the south side of Vladislav Hall, the Ludvík Wing rose during the early 1620s, its bulk projected into the terraced garden. It contained the offices of the Bohemian Chamber, the Bohemian Chancellery, and, during the reign of Rudolph II, when Prague was the Emperor's principal seat, the Imperial Chancellery. In a second-floor room – at the level of Vladislav Hall – is the famous window from which the Governors representing Emperor Matthias were hurled on May 23, 1618, a "defenestration" that precipitated the Thirty Years' War.

On the east side of the Old Royal Palace stands the Hall of the Diet, where equally dramatic events took place. Here, under the dense net vault created by the royal architect Bonifaz Wohlmut between 1559 and 1563, the Supreme Court and the Diet held their sessions. The records – the statute books and the land rolls – of these two supreme bodies of the Bohemian Estates were kept in the New Land Rolls, which occupied a parallel wing above the Riders Staircase.

The New Royal Palace

By the 16th century it had become clear that so many rooms within the Old Royal Palace had been given over to official and state functions that the ruler could no longer live there. Soon after Archduke Ferdinand of Tyrol became Governor of Prague in 1547 he commissioned what he called a "new building" for himself alongside the White Tower at the southern end of the present-day wing between the second and third courtyards. This fairly modest structure could

not compete with the nearby Renaissance palaces of the Rosenberg and Pernstein families; nevertheless, it would serve as the foundation of the New Royal Palace. When Rudolph II chose Prague as his permanent place of residence, he naturally became concerned about the site of his Imperial seat. The Bohemian Estates, which had been trying to persuade the reigning monarch to establish himself in Prague ever since the Habsburgs gained the Bohemian throne, immediately authorized the Emperor to levy a special tax to finance the repair and completion of his residence. At the same time, the revenue also made it possible to begin construction on the new royal domicile. This was the so-called "summer house," which adjoined Archduke Ferdinand's building and faced south towards the town, and the Emperor made it the comfortable home he sought in Prague. From the building a covered passage made of wood led past the dwelling of the dowager Empress and the royal kitchens to the Old Royal Palace. However, most of the construction work occurred around what is now the second courtyard, which became a ceremonial area. Above the Romanesque wall, between the second and third courtyards, the so-called Rudolph Gallery was commenced during the reign of Maximilian II. A spacious, three-story structure, it would, beginning in the 1590s, contain Rudolph II's collections and treasury. In the late part of the same decade the northern wing of the New Royal Palace, built over the Powder Bridge, also reached completion. Here, above the new stables, in what is today the Picture Gallery of Prague Castle, the New and Spanish Halls were erected, both of them for ceremonial purposes. From these chambers another wooden passage led to the northern precincts of the great castle complex,

the site of a zoo, a pheasantry, a riding school, and the Royal Gardens, the latter a setting for two Ball Games Courts and the Summer Palace. Such was the castle through which the enigmatic Emperor walked, using the covered passages while seeking solitude as well as relief, from the drudgery and boredom of his political duties, in the creative activity of his circle of scientists, craftsmen, and artists.

The later Habsburg Emperors did not live in Prague, which left the castle more or less abandoned except for limited visits by the monarch or members of his court. Still, Ferdinand III, like Rudolph II, had a new palace erected within the castle complex, on the site of the southern wing of the second courtyard.

On the right, below the balcony, is the entrance to the Chancellery and reception rooms of the President of the Czech Republic, all situated in a wing designed by Nicolo Pacassi in the Classical style and dating from 1755–62.

The façade of the present entrance to the Old Royal Palace faces the third courtyard. It was designed in the mid-18th century by Nicolo Pacassi in a style appropriate to its royal surroundings.

Following this brief flurry of new construction, Prague Castle would see no further building activity for some decades. Finally, in 1755–75 the Viennese architect Nicolo Pacassi embarked on a major conversion project designed to give the exterior of the royal enclave a uniform look, marked by cold Classical façades generally characteristic of European palace architecture of the period. Centered upon the third courtyard, this campaign would introduce the stately portal with its balcony and its torchbearers created by the sculptor Ignác Platzer. The wing now houses the presidential offices and state rooms. The western precincts of the castle received a new ceremonial courtyard, today known as the first courtyard, the scene of official receptions for foreign delegations and, more recently, lunchtime concerts given by the band of the castle guard. The south wing is used as a guest house for state visitors.

Prague Castle underwent its last major alteration in the 1920s, when it was modified in keeping with the needs of the President of the Czechoslovak Republic. Directed by the Laibach architect Joze Plecnik, the alterations mainly affected the interior of the castle.

While the Old Royal Palace serves primarily as an historical monument, where state ceremonies are staged from time to time, the newer parts of the castle are alive with the activities of the President of the Czech Republic. Thus, Prague Castle remains the seat of a national government, at the same time that, under President Václav Havel, it has become an ever-more lively center of culture, complete with halls for concerts and exhibitions.

The Riders' Staircase under whose magnificant star vaulting tournament participants would ride their horse into Vladislav Hall.

opposite: *Antonín Braun's personification of Night, a bronze of 1733 installed before the Ball Games Court, which dates from 1567.*

The Spanish Hall (known as the
New Hall until the end of
the 17th century) dates from
1604–06, when Giovanni Maria Filippi
built it as Rudoph II's Treasury
in the New Palace. The sculptural
frieze reflects the style achieved
during the reign of Rudolph II.
In 1748, Kilian Ignaz Dientzenhofer
increased the height of the room
to the level of the roof truss.
The stucco work between the
two cornices dates from
the same building campaign.

right: The large mirrors on
the left date from the 1836 coronation
of Ferdinand V. In 1865–68 the preparations
for the coronation of Franz Joseph I,
which never took place, were the final
changes made in this hall. In addition to
the chandeliers, they involved the allegorical
statues in niches designed by A.P. de Vigne.

The House of the Lords of Kunstatt

Just a few steps from Husova the house numbered 222 incorporates the ground floor of a Romanesque palace erected during the eventful last decades of the 12th century. The street, formerly known as Dominican, was one of the major transport routes of the Old Town, which Vyšehrad, a much frequented thoroughfare in the Middle Ages, used to traverse. At this time the palace was one of the emergent city's most splendid patrician residences. The builder, although unknown for certain, has been hypothetically identified as Smil von Kirchschlag, an important player in Bohemian politics during the final years of the 12th century and an ancestor of the rich and powerful Lichtenburg family.

The aristocratic Kunstatts, after whom the house is named, lived here in the last third of the 14th century, but the first reliable references date from the year 1406, when the dwelling was described as *curia dominis Boczkonis.* The said Boczko happened to be the grandfather of the great (and fat) Bohemian King George of Kunstatt and Poděbrady (1420–71), who however resided not here but rather in the royal court next to the so-called "shabby" city gate, later to become the Powder Tower. Today, the massively vaulted rooms of the Kunstatt house serve as exhibition halls for the Prague Department of Monuments.

Once the ground floor of a 12th-century house, this Romanesque hall is now the basement.

opposite: *The courtyard of what is now house no. 222.*

The Royal Summer Palace

(Belvedere)

When Ferdinand I (r. 1526–64) ascended the throne of Bohemia he brought with him tastes acquired during his life among the sophisticated and pampered aristocracy of the Netherlands. Thus, he was one of the first monarchs to promote the Renaissance in Prague. Meanwhile, his background also made him impatient with the Royal Palace, which he found too constricting and uncomfortable. Despite his limited financial resources and the political interests that drew him to Vienna more than to Prague, which he rarely visited, the young King launched upon a campaign to expand the palace. At the same time, he had a new "Italian" garden laid out north of the Stag Moat, where he also commissioned a summer palace for his ailing wife, Queen Anna. In 1537 Paolo della Stella and his Italian masons began work on the so-called Belvedere, its airy Ionic loggia, decorated with bas-reliefs of mythological scenes, surrounding a series of spacious rooms within. The Renaissance arcades are crowned with a relief-carved frieze dating from 1540.

Rising above the slender elements of an arcade reminiscent of sunny Italy, the green roof of the Summer Palace, or Belvedere, has been a landmark of Renaissance Prague since the mid-16th century.

On Stella's death, the royal architect Bonifaz Wohlmut completed the Summer Palace, adding the first story above and a copper-clad roof shaped like an overturned ships hull. The royal family had their splendidly furnished rooms on the ground floor (where they were plundered by the Swedish Army in 1648), which left the upper floor free for a ballroom and the royal picture gallery. The King saw the Summer Palace completed in 1563, just one year before he died. While his successor Maximilian II preferred to live in Vienna, his grandson Rudolph II appreciated not only Prague but also the Summer Palace, which came to be known as the Belvedere only in the 19th century. Rudolph liked especially to linger in this part of the Royal Gardens.

The "Singing Fountain,"
cast in 1564 by the bell-founder
Thomas Jaros for the Royal Gardens
laid out before the Summer Palace.

Following its misuse for military purposes during the Empire, the Summer Palace was restored to new life in the 1830s, when Count Chotek, Burgrave of Prague, had the overgrown gardens below the Belvedere replanted and opened as a public park, the first such facility in the Bohemian capital. Meanwhile, the Prague art union made plans to embellish the Summer Palace with large paintings, a program that finally became a reality in 1851. Still devoted to the visual arts, the Belvedere is a venue for exhibitions organized by the Chancellery and drawn from artists all over the world.

The "History of Bohemia," a cycle of paintings executed in the 1860s by Kristian Ruben and his pupils. They hang in the upstairs galleries of the Belvedere or Summer Palace.

At the Summer Palace the long western loggia designed and built by Paolo della Stella constitutes one of the purest examples of Italian Renaissance architecture north of the Alps.

Schwarzenberg Palace

On the south side of Castle Square (Hradčanské náměstí) stand two palaces bearing the name of the Franconian/Bohemian Schwarzenberg family. The larger and older of the patrician dwellings, situated next to the former Barnabite monastery, came into being after the great fire of 1541, when King Ferdinand I gave  four of the burnt-out sites in Castle Square to the Lord High Chamberlain Jan the Younger, Baron von Lobkovicz, who became Supreme Burgrave in 1544. From 1545 to 1567 Baron Jan kept the Italian architect "Augustinus" (no doubt Agostino Galli) busy erecting a magnificent residence in the Renaissance fortress style of the Northern Italy. Old Prague could boast only one other aristocratic dwelling of comparable splendor: the palace of the Lords of Rosenberg situated within the castle complex and already renovated and modernized in 1556. But come the 18th century, when the Rosenberg mansion got swallowed up by the rather amorphous pile of the Institute of Noblewomen, the palace of the Schwarzenberg Princes – their title inherited from the Princes of Eggenerg in 1719 – remained the finest example of secular Renaissance architecture in Prague.

Stepped gables, decorated with sgraffitoed "Venetian" plant motifs, crown three wings of the mansion above a huge cavetto cornice broken by lunettes. The wings enclose a courtyard separated from Castle Square by a wall that is also decorated with sgraffito and a row of little gable-like crenellations. The exterior is equally famous for the trompe-l'oeil diamond-point rustication painted over virtually very surface below the cornice. One of the loveliest views of Prague is available from the terrace on the south side of the great house.

The inhabitants of Schwarzenberg Palace included the all-too-ambitious Georg von Lobkovicz, the Lord High Steward who so desperately aspired to the office of Supreme Burgrave that he alarmed his opponents. These in turn charged Lord Georg with conspiracy before the Emperor, who ordered the accused placed under house arrest for the remainder of his life. Having confiscated Schwarzenberg Palace, Rudolph II gave it in 1600 to Petr Vok von Rosenberg, the famous book collector, patron of the arts, and opposition politician, in exchange for the latter's palace in the castle precinct.

In the years 1945 – 93 Schwarzenberg Palace housed the Military History Museum, installed under wood ceilings painted in 1580 with motifs from antiquity by an unknown Prague master. Now the monumental rooms await new tenants.

A collection of old cannons installed in the courtyard of Schwarzenberg Palace.

Hrzán Palace

Visitors arriving in Loretto Street (Loretánská) from Castle Square will be struck by a splendid Renaissance house directly opposite the barracks of the castle guards situated in the former palace of Georg Adam II, Count von Martinicz. Earlier, in the 14th century, this was the site of the house occupied by Peter Parler, a native of Swabia who gained international renown as the builder of St. Vitus's Cathedral. Under Rudolph II the narrow lanes of Hradčany near Prague Castle became a fashionable place of residence for courtiers, officials, and ambassadors. The house at number 177 originally belonged to the Lords of Plauen, before being taken over by Adam von Sternberg the Elder, the chief tax collector of Bohemia. Later, the property fell into the hands of the merchant Jan Rebenik. In 1601 it was bought by Ulrich Desiderius Pruskovsky von Pruckov, the Lord Chamberlain, who converted the dwelling into a typical Renaissance mansion. In 1657 the Lord Chamberlain acquired another house, this one on the steep slope above Uvoz, where it

Here, the Baroque façade glows in the darkness, thanks to a formerly gaslit street lamp typical of Prague Castle.

reaches a height of three stories below the level of Lorentánská. He then had the building converted to form a courtyard wing, with stables erected below the courtyard. In the second half of the 17th century the property belonged to the Counts of Kolowrat-Krakowsky, and in 1708 it was purchased by Sigismund Hrzán von Harras, who initiated a new conversion. Finally, during the second half of the 18th century, the house reverted to the cathedral chapter, became the deanery, and acquired the beautiful Late Baroque façade that survives today.

Today the salons of Hrzán Palace are used by the Czech government for ceremonies and receptions.

Martinicz Palace

One of the finest Renaissance palaces within the vicinity of Prague Castle is the residence built in the third quarter of the 16th century by the Lord Chamberlain Andreas Teyfl von Kinsdorf. The cost of erecting the quadrangular mansion proved so onerous that as soon as it was completed, in 1589, His Lordship had

no choice but to sell the property to Georg Borita, Baron von Martinicz. The new owner belonged to an aristocratic family of Bohemian Catholics, a clan known to history for Jaroslav Borita von Martinicz, one of the Imperial Governors thrown from a window (defenestrated) of the Court Chancellery in Prague Castle on May 23, 1618, by Protestant representatives of the Bohemian Estates. It was this act of violent rebellion against Habsburg domination that triggered the Thirty Years' War. After the Catholic faction succeeded in putting down the insurgency, Baron Martinicz, who miraculously survived his 55-foot fall into the castle moat, where he landed on a dung heap, began to refurbish his residence on the Hradčany during the 1620s. The structure itself would remain simple, its exterior décor limited to the courtyard, where sgraffito depicted the Labors of Hercules and the Life of Samson. Laden with titles and powers – not only Count but also Supreme Burgrave of Prague, Burgrave of Karlstein, Councillor or Governor, Lord Chamberlain, Lord Marshall, and Lord High

above: *Portrait bust of a Bohemian Queen carved in alabaster by an unknown artist.*

opposite: *The great house, with its exterior walls decorated with sgraffito, survives as one of the jewels of Renaissance Prague.*

Steward in the Kingdom of Bohemia – Jaroslav von Martinicz had his personal coat of arms imposed upon the Renaissance portal, the external façade decorated with Biblical scenes (sgraffito narrating the Life of Joseph), and another floor added on, complete with Mannerist gables. Still, he focused mainly on the interior, where, for the large hall on the piano nobile, he commissioned a large-scale ceiling

fresco, known today only through old drawings. However, all that survives of this ensemble are the colorfully painted wood ceilings in the anterooms. Later covered by brickwork, they did not return to light until the entire building was restored in 1971 as offices for the municipal architects of Prague. Now the ceilings can be enjoyed by everyone who attends the concerts of early music regularly held here.

below: The sgraffitoed decorations applied to the exterior walls of Martinicz Palace make this mansion a pearl among the Renaissance dwellings of Prague. One cycle of decorations is devoted to the Labors of Hercules, another to the Life of St. Joseph.

opposite: Painted ceillings executed in the 17th century and recovered in recent times.

Waldstein Palace

Albrecht von Waldstein (Wallenstein) is known to history as a brilliant, ambitious and ruthless general, who invaded northern Germany and later sucessfully fought against the Swedes. He even aspired to the throne of Bohemia, taking unparalleled advantage of the shifts in power that occurred during the awful Thirty Years' War. A member of one of the older Bohemian families and a grim presence in his portraits, Count Waldstein discovered his great opportunity after he led the Catholic forces to victory at the Battle of the White Mountain in 1620. From the confiscations that followed, he acquired some sixty estates in northern and northeastern Bohemia, administering them according to the needs of his military enterprises. In this way he found a source of capital with which to construct not only a palace in Prague but also a château on the lands of his Friedland duchy in Jicín.

The grandiose palace was the first Baroque residence in Prague and probably the first such edifice built to compete with the Royal Palace. It stood below the Hradčany on a site once occupied by twenty-five earlier houses, three gardens, a lime kiln, and a portal. Although erected by Italians under the direction of the fortress-builder Giovanni Pieroni over a period of six years (1624–30), Waldstein Palace would reflect the owner's taste in a variety of ways. The building, for instance, is a self-enclosed, self-regarding, isolated domain at the center of town, separated from the urban environment by thick walls and a square in front. The main façade, largely influenced by Dutch architecture, looks onto Valdštejnské náměstí.

The apotheosis of Albrecht von Waldstein constitutes a theme pursued throughout the palace. The Knights' Hall, one of the handsomest rooms in the mansion (a space presently used for concerts), is crowned by a ceiling fresco portaying Waldstein as the god Mars riding across the heavens in a triumphal chariot. A two-story chapel dedicated to St. Wenceslas, the patron saint of Count Waldstein, is painted with scenes of the saint's life. Other rooms reflect the Waldstein belief in astral matters, among them the Astronomy Gallery decorated with personifications of the seven planets, zodaical signs, allegories of the seasons, and the corners of the globe. Along with a profusion of paintings, Oriental carpets, Italian furniture, and Bohemian glass, the palace rooms were all furnished with splendid tapestries and hangings embellished with the heraldic colors of the Duchy of Friedland.

The three great arches of the sala terrena open out from the palace into a Mannerist garden that was extremely spacious for the times. This "garden room," even though an intimate, private space, is the most brilliantly original part of the palace and may very well have been inspired by the cathedral loggia in Leghorn. In 1859 Schiller's *Wallenstein* was performed here, under the vault decorated by Bianco with theatrically clad figures from the *Aeneid*. During summer the sala terrena is still a venue for good music.

The main promenade of the garden features bronze copies of statues by Adriaen de Vries, a

sculptor at Rudolph IIs court who had returned to Prague at Waldstein's request. Since 1648 the originals have stood in the gardens of Drottningholm Place in Stockholm. Behind a pond at the foot of Waldstein's garden, which had both a grotto and an aviary, Nicolo Sebregondi built a spacious riding school, a structure now used as an exhibition space.

The Waldstein family owned the palace until 1945. In the early 1950s, it was still occupied, with "gracious permission" of the new rulers, by the hundred-year-old Countess Marie Waldstein. Today the property houses the Ministry of Culture, the Conservation Office, and the Museum of Education.

58

Most of the rooms in Walstein Palace
were redecorated in a more sober manner during
the 19th century. However, the Knights' Hall
survives in all its glorification
of Count Waldstein. Indeed, the ceiling fresco
by Baccio Bianco shows the hero chariot-racing
across the heavens as the god Mars.

59

Michna Palace

At the end of the 16th century the knight Jan Vchynsk (from the family later known as Kinsky) commissioned the court architect Ulrico Aostalli to build an interesting summer house, situated below the Petřín Hill vineyards on the south side of the Lesser Town (Malá Strana) in Karmelitská. The property then changed ownership and at one point came into the hands of Count Heinrich Matthias von Turn und Valsassina, the leading figure of the opposition party within the Bohemian Estates. In 1623 the summer house was bought by a man who may have been the most ruthless parvenu among all the new power players. This was Paul Albert Michna von Waczynov, a onetime minor Chancellery secretary, of unknown bourgeois origins, who later became Count Michna von Waizenhofen, wealthy from his role as supply officer to the Imperial Army.

The new owner radically modified the banqueting hall in the northern part of the summer house, removing the painted ceiling and adding a story. Very likely he also began to build the riding school and a supply store, but met with an early death in 1632. Although his son Václav also failed to complete the conversion, he did create a unique private garden, entered, as at Waldstein Palace, through the most splendid part of the mansion. The work of an unknown Italian architect, the central bay of the Mannerist façade giving onto the garden evokes the Villa Pamphili in Rome and thus brings a note of pure Italian Renaissance to Prague. Also worth remarking is the wealth of stucco decoration, both within the palace and outside, executed by Giovanni Domenico Galli in the years 1644–45.

The next owners of Michna Palace also came from the high nobility, first the Sinzendorf Counts, who acquired the property in 1678, and then, in 1684, the Counts von Schwarzenberg, who had the park laid out in the French style, a project completed in 1720. After the middle of the century, however, the palace went through some rough times, beginning in 1767, when the Treasury took over Michna Palace, using it first as an arsenal and then as a military command post. In 1921 the Sokol athletics club bought the mansion and converted it. After serving as a sports college from 1951 to 1990, Michna Palace returned to the Sokol and presently houses a sports museum.

Michna Palace, originally built in the Mannerist style, faces away from the busy Karmelitská towards an imposing garden, where the mansions façade is notable for its distinctive central pavilion.

At Michna Palace a rusticated portal with modern grillework by F. Krásn (opposite) leads visitors from the Karmelitská into the forecourt, which retains elements of the original Renaissance summer house (left).

Lobkovicz Palace

(Hradčany)

Housed within Lobkovicz Palace close by the Black Tower is one of the attractions most frequented by visitors to Prague Castle: the collections of the National History Museum. Here, in the southeast precinct of Hradcany, Jaroslav von Pernstein, from one of the oldest and most powerful families in Bohemia, built his grandiose residence on the site of structures destroyed by the terrible fire of 1541. It was, however, Jaroslav's brother Vratislav, the "ostentatious" Lord Chancellor of Bohemia, who, after 1570, oversaw the second phase of work on the mansion. Today, all that remains of the original Renaissance building are a few architectural and decorative details, such as bits of terra-cotta and sgraffito dating from 1576. With the marriage of Polyxena von Pernstein, the Spanish-educated, cultured daughter of the old Chancellor, to the similarly civilized Zdenko Adalbert Popel von Lobkovicz, the palace passed to an extremely important and wealthy noble clan, in whose possession it remained until 1945.

In 1651 Lobkovicz Palace underwent renovation in the Baroque manner, from designs by Carlo Lurago, a campaign undertaken by Zdenko Adalbert's son, Prince Václav Eusebius von Lobkovicz, who in 1669 would become President of the Privy Council under Emperor Leopold I. During the 1660s this grandee kept the masons and stucco

St. Wenceslas, *an altarpiece painted by Peter Brandl in 1723 for the chapel in Lobkovicz Palace.*

opposite: *Lobkovicz Palace from one of the two portals of the Black Tower that constitute the eastern gateway to the Hradčany.*

*In Lobkovicz Palace, the ceiling
over the dining hall painted
in 1665–69 by Fabian Václav Harovnáik.*

*Castle guards patrolling in front
of Lobkovicz Palace, with the Black Tower
looming in the background.*

workers Giovanni Galli and Giovanni B. Pozzo, together with the painter Fabian Václav Harovnáik, busy decorating the ceilings of the main hall and several other rooms. Of this program, all that remains are the ceilings in the chapel (Life of St. Wenceslas), the dining hall (mythological scenes), and the vestibule (Triumph of Caesar). The chapel also retains an altar painting by Peter Brandl. In its present form, Lobkovicz Place dates from 1810, when a new and radical renovation left the street façade with only two pilastered portals from the original construction. In the 1970s Lobkovicz Palace took on new life following its restoration and the installation of the historical "treasure."

Nostitz Palace

The Nostitz family from Lausitz arrived in Bohemia shortly before the outbreak of the Thirty Years' War and then remained to play leading roles in the cultural history of the country, from the 17th century through the 19th. The Supreme Burgrave Johann Hartwig, Count von Nostitz-Rieneck, was the first of his family to settle permanently in Prague, where he began erecting a spacious new palace in 1662. The quadrangular structure rose on the border between the Maltese district, an area close by the Lesser Town banks of the Vltava, and the Garden of Lazarus, terrain that had been divided up only shortly before. In a manner characteristic of the Baroque, the mansion is a grandiose, freestanding structure that rises imposingly above the adjacent town houses. Unlike the Mannerist Waldstein and Michna Palaces, it does not face away from the town; on the contrary, it both marks and dominates Maltese Square (Maltézské náměstí). The plain façade, designed by an unknown Italian architect (perhaps Francesco Caratti), is rhythmically articulated by twelve giant Palladian pilasters, the first of their kind in Prague, since the Czernín Palace, with its famous façade of sculpted columns, had yet to be erected.

Subsequently, as Prague moved from the Late Baroque Age into the Rococo, the Nostitz Palace façade acquired a more "pleasing" character. Around 1720 appeared the balustrade with four figures of antique military leaders, sculptures created by

Ferdinand Maximilian Brokoff. The portal was added in 1760. Meanwhile, on the interior, Václav Bernhard Ambrozi frescoed the hall (Helios on his chariot) and the ceiling above the stairs in 1757. Eight years later Count Franz Anton von Nostitz-Rieneck, took over his fathers residence, from which he served as patron of the Estates Theater (initially called the Nostitz Theater) in the Fruit Market (Ovocný trh). Shortly thereafter, he commissioned Thomas Haffenecker to convert part of the garden into a riding school, while also extending the palace

Nostitz Palace is entered from Maltese Square through a column-flanked portal designed by the sculptor Thomas Haffenecker in 1760.

The National Gallery many years ago acquired most of the Dutch paintings in the Nostitz collection, one of the largest such hoards in Prague.

Václav Bernhard Ambrozis stuccos and paintings were commissioned by Count Franz Anton von Nostitz-Rieneck, patron of the Estates Theater, after he inherited Nostitz Palace in 1765.

gardens as far as the Vltava. In them he built a summer house for his son's teacher, Josef Dobrovsk, later known as an expert Slavist and historian.

Much acclaimed, the Nostitz collections were started by Count Otto the Younger, an uncle of Johann Hartwig. In the 19th century the picture gallery was thought to contain the most important private collection in Prague. Housed in the palace until 1945, it now forms the core of the Dutch painting collection in the National Gallery. The extensive library assembled in Nostitz Palace remains there, albeit administered by the National Museum.

Czernín Palace

O verriding ambition accounts for the pharaonic magnitude of Czernín Palace, begun in 1669 by Humprecht Jan, Count Czernín von Chudenitz. Born into a family of passionate art collectors much under the influence of Venice, Count Czernín typified the Baroque era in his eagerness to construct a residence splendid enough to rival the Royal Palace in Hradčany. Behind the 150-meter-long façade, with its colonnade of thirty two-story pilasters, stands a palace on which four generations of builders worked, without ever realizing the full extent of Count Czerníns conception.

Francesco Caratti, the original architect, introduced the Mannerist scale of the exterior and the Palladian motifs applied to it. He also designed the basic structure, but left details to his successors, Giovanni Baptista Maderna and Domenico Egidio Rossi, who remained with the project until 1697. They also completed the large gallery, which became a "treasure house" for the picture collection begun by Count Czernín during his four-year tenure (1661–64) as Imperial Ambassador in Venice. Once installed in Czernín Palace, the collection had no equal in Prague and thus attracted many visitors.

After 1718 the architect Franz Maximilian Kaňka continued the project, building a monumental stairway that took up the entire area between the two inner courtyards. On the ceiling Václav Lorenz Reiner painted a fascinating version of

the Battle of the Titans, whose original colors, unfortunately, could not be restored after the scene had been painted over in the 19th century. West of the palace, Kaňka designed the French garden and the two tall arcades of its loggia. Alongside the loggia this artist also erected a circular salon with stuccos based on motifs by Jacques Callot. In 1726 the area in front of Czernín Palace was finally cleared, which allowed the world to take in the incredible vastness of the façade.

During the wars of the Austrian succession Czernín Palace suffered considerable damage. But following the French occupation, the architect Anselmo Lurago was commissioned to give the plain rear façade a lighter, more lyrical touch by adding three sets of arcades. Still, the wars continued, and in 1757 the Prussians inflicted further damage on the great pile. By this time the Czernín family could no longer afford to live in their palace. In 1796–1809 it housed the picture gallery of the Society of Patriotic Art Lovers. Next the building served as a hospital, with worse to come after 1851, when the government bought the property and turned it into a barracks.

In 1919 the young Czech Republic decided to make Czernín Palace the seat of its Foreign Ministry, which had the architect Pavel Janák restore the mansion and gardens in a very sensitive manner, a project carried out in 1928–34. As the home of the Foreign Ministry, the old Czernín dwelling witnessed one of the tragic consequences of the Communist takeover. On March 10, 1948, the Foreign Minister, Jan Masaryk, the son of the revered first President of the Czech Republic, was found dead at the foot of the palace, whether from suicide or from defenestration remains a mystery. Only recently has the Ministry building regained some of its former splendor and importance.

opposite: *The long passageways of the Early Baroque Cernin Palace were among the first spaces in Prague specifically designed to exhibit paintings.*

below: *Thirty colossal engaged Corinthian columns mark of the 490-foot-long façade of Cernin Palace. In the first quarter of the 18th century, the architect Franz Maximilian Kaňka relieved the severe monumentality of the great façade with a gracefully projecting portico.*

overleaf: *In the 1920s the architect Pavel Janák renovated this spacious foyer, at the end of which stands the niched sculpture* Music *by Josef Václav Myslbek.*

75

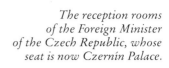
*The reception rooms
of the Foreign Minister
of the Czech Republic, whose
seat is now Czernín Palace.*

In Czernín Palace,
Pavel Janák also modernized
the grand staircase
in a suitably auspicious
yet sensitive manner.

Kolowrat-Novohradsky Palace

Until recently this noble house in the Old Town Fruit Market (Ovocný trh) languished as one of the forgotten residences of the Prague aristocracy. Its worth finally became apparent during the recent reconstruction of the Estates Theater, for which the palace now serves as the administrative office. It also houses a small studio theater created in the attic.

The building is nothing more than the torso of the palatial establishment built by Count Jan Václav von Kolowrat-Novohradsky (1638–90). In 1673, when construction began, no theater stood on the site, which left more space in front of the palace. There was also far more space behind, with the result that the quadrangular mansion and its gardens could extend their domain all the way to the city moat. The *sala terrena* survived until 1927, by which time the Old Town palace gardens had completely disappeared.

Today all that remains of this Kolowrat residence is the street façade, behind which Count Franz Anton von Kolowrat-Novohradsky hung his important collection of prints and drawings at the end of the 18th century. This nobleman was the last of his line but also the first president of the Society of Patriotic Art Lovers. Stylistically, his family palace is unique in Prague, its long, horizontal façade more reminiscent of Vienna's Palais Montecuccoli than of patrician dwellings in the Bohemian capital. This may be explained by the Viennese origins of the presumed architect, Giovanni Domenico Orsi, who, beginning

in 1660, worked for the Prague Old Town masons' guild. Now that it has been restored, the delicate architecture of Kolowrat-Novohradsky Palace constitutes one of the newest "sights" in Prague.

*Wooden ceilings colorfully
painted in the 17th century
still adorn the refurbished rooms
of Kolowrat-Novohradsky Palace.*

81

below: *The main entryway to Kolowrat-Novohradsky Palace with the Kolowrat arms prominently displayed above the portal.*

right: *Classic beauty characterizes Kolowrat-Novohradsky Palace, an aristocratic dwelling erected in 1673. The long façade – so reminiscent of Vienna's aristocratic palais – is presumed to have been designed by Giovanni Domenico Orsi.*

above: *The main façade
of Kolowrat-Novorhadsky Palace
looks onto the Estates' Theater,
for which the renovated mansion now
serves as an administrative office.*

Troja Palace

Between 1678 and 1691 Count Václav Adalbert von Sternberg, had a magnificent country villa built on his Zadní Ovenec estate north of Prague. In 1989, following twelve years of reconstruction, the great house returned to civilization in all its original glory. However, the

restoration raised a number of questions, such as why had Count Sternberg desired such an imposing residence in an economically insignificant place somewhat remote from Prague and difficult of access? The answer lies partly in the overall historical context, which found the Bohemian nobility eager to upgrade Prague as a royal seat and thus persuade the King/Emperor to live there. The Royal Orchard happened to lie close by the site of Count Sternberg's country mansion, which the builder designed as a comfortable refuge and place of refreshment for a royal hunting party foraging through the orchard. This can be deduced from a number of symbolic features, among them the main axis of the palace, which is built on a man-made terrace and so orientated that it faces Hradčany. Moreover, the program of frescoes in the Grand Hall is a vast pictorial homage to the House of Habsburg. Also supporting the hypothesis are certain practical features, such as the exceptional capacity of the wine cellars.

The French architect Jean-Baptiste Mathey designed the villa, possibly taking as his model the Villa Altieri in Rome. However, it seems to have been built by Domenico Orsi, Silvestro Carloni, and perhaps even Christoph Dientzenhofer. The focus of the architectural ensemble falls powerfully on the central structure, which houses the Grand Hall, a two-story chamber reached by the sweeping double ramps of an oval staircase richly adorned with figure sculptures representing the victory of the Olympian Gods over the Titans, the sons of Mother Earth. Two Titans serve as caryatids enslaved to support the upper landing, their two brothers having already been hurled into the Tartarus. Meanwhile, the Olympians stand triumphant atop the balustrade. Although inspired by Gianlorenzo Bernini, this ambitious composition was created by two sculptors from Dresden, Johann Georg Heermann and his nephew Paul.

The immense program of frescoes decorating the Grand Hall is attributed to a pair of Flemish painters, the brothers Abraham and Isaak Godyn of Antwerp, who completed the work shortly after the Zenta victory (1697), taking account of the anti-Turkish feelings of the time. Over the fireplace, Emperor Leopold I stands triumphant in Classical garb, while on the opposite wall the Legend of Babenberg unfolds. On the lateral walls as well the Habsburg's parade before the viewer: Charles V renouncing the throne on one side and the marriage of his parents, Philip I and Joanna of Castille, on the other. Meanwhile, the ceiling opens to the heavens in virtuoso trompe-loeil glorifying the victory of Austria and its allies over the pagan enemy. Other rooms display frescoes by Francesco Marchetti, and there are paintings even in the stables, executed by Abraham Godyn.

Equally interesting is the palace setting, especially the gardens, which have been carefully reconstructed from old engravings, complete with terra-cotta vases, a large fountain, an orchard, and paths leading to picturesque views.

*From above the fireplace
Abraham Godyns painting of Justice
gazes down on the assembled company
in the Grand Hall at Troja Palace.*

85

right: *At Troja Palace,*
the monumental horseshoe stairway
leading from the garden to the Grand Hall
within the central pavilion of Troja Palace was built
in 1683 and adorned with massive
figure sculptures representing the victory
of the Olympian Gods over the Titans.

Troja Palace now houses part of the collection of paintings owned by the city of Prague, especially works by 19th-century Czech artists. The palace has also become a prime venue for concerts, and good wine can be had in the former coach house.

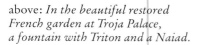

above: *In the beautiful restored*
French garden at Troja Palace,
a fountain with Triton and a Naiad.

above: *The rooms of the piano nobile*
are decorated with ceiling paintings of
mythological subjects by Francesco Marchetti.

90

The interior of Troja Palace
was restored during the 1980s
in preparation for opening
the great house to the public.

One of the smaller rooms in
Troja Palace used for exhibitions.
It includes a tiled stove as well as
a fresco by Francesco Marchetti.

This salon in Troja Palace
has been decorated with wall paintings
representing Chinese landscapes,
all executed by Johann Adam Delsenbach.

93

Toscana Palace

he massive Toscana Palace dominates the west side of Castle Square (Hradčanské náměstí). So grandiose is the building that it forms a kind of architectural pendant to the New Royal Palace. Thanks to the broad façade, the lanes on either side are exceptionally narrow. At first Toscana Palace would appear so self-centered as to be indifferent to the surrounding public space. However, at the entrance to Loretto Street (Loretánská), which almost every visitor passes through, there stands a splendid statue of the Archangel Michael brandishing his flaming sword. Modeled by the sculptor Ottavio Mosto, the figure was installed by the builder of Toscana Palace, Count Michael Oswald von Thun und Hohenstein, whose patron saint was Michael. His family, originally from the South Tyrol, endowed Prague with many buildings during the Baroque era.

By the time he built Toscana Palace in 1689–91, towards the end of his life, Count Michael had become one of the wealthiest landowners in Bohemia. The design for the mansion was prepared by Jean-Baptiste Mathey, a Burgundian who had studied in Rome and then found great success in Prague. The two tower-like pavilions with which he crowned Toscana Palace recall Italian villas, while the balustrade with statues running between them clearly found their model in the Villa Medici. The figures came from the workshop of Jan Brokoff. Even more important decorative features are the two identical portals composed as flanking pairs of

above: *Ottavio Mostos statue of the Archangel Michael surveys passersby from the corner of Loretánská. Michael was the patron saint of the Count von Thun who built Toscana Palace.*

opposite: *One of the twin entryways through the main façade of Toscana Palace (late 17th century). The arms of the Grands Dukes of Tuskany crown the pediment above the balcony.*

smooth columns with Ionic capitals supporting balconies overhung with huge cartouches framing the arms of the Thun family. Only rarely in Prague does a palatial façade boast twin entryways.

In 1718 Princess Anna Maria von Sachsen-Lauenburg, the wife of the last Medici Grand Duke of Tuscany, acquired the property and moved in. In 1741, during the wars of the Austrian succession, Princess Anna Maria received univited guests when Frances Maréchal Bellisle decided to make Toscana Palace his headquarters. Her daughter Anna Maria, from a first marriage to Philipp Wilhelm von Pfalz-Neuburg, took the palace as her dowry when she married Prince Ferdinand Maria of Bavaria, a brother of Emperor Charles VII. As a result, the Zweibrücken branch of the Bavarian Wittelsbach family owned the palace until 1805, when it came into the possession of Archduke Ferdinand, who assumed the title of Grand Duke of Tuscany in 1814. Today Tuscana Palace is used by the Czech Foreign Ministry.

The monumental façade
of Toscana Palace forms
the western end of Hradčany
or Castle Square.

Liechtenstein Palace

(Kampa Island)

The story of this patrician dwelling began in the 1650s when Jan de la Cron, a Dutch immigrant who had become Royal Military Advisor, Sergeant General of the Cavalry, and Commander in Chief of Prague, managed to acquire several attractive properties both quickly and cheaply. In this he typified a new group of opportunistic military officials active in Prague immediately after the Thirty Years' War. Specifically, Jan bought two houses in the Lesser Town Square (Malostranské náměstí) together with a garden on nearby

Kampa Island. A generation later, in 1684–96, his South Austrian son-in-law, Franz Helfried, Baron von Kaiserstein, had a Baroque palazzetto erected in the western part of the garden. In the years since, the building has been converted so often that it retains little of what originally must have been considerable charm.

In many respects, the structure was unique in Prague. Not only did the main façade, with its two pavilion-like towers, look onto the water, but, in addition, the plan was hexagonal on the outside and octagonal on the inside. Although not known for certain, the architect was probably Giovanni Baptista Alliprandi, who would later build Kaiserstein Palace as well.

The extensive garden on the banks of the Vltava also became one of the sights of 18th-century Prague. Always lovely, with its original ponds and beds of carnations, it evolved into one of the most beautiful gardens in the Bohemian capital.

A tiled stove with 19th-century ornamentation.

During the 19th century the palace on the Vltava underwent several transformations, beginning with its acquisition by the Prince of Liechtenstein, who had the place fitted out in the Empire style. The next owner, the Prague miller Frantisek Odkolek, altered the structure even more profoundly when, in 1864, he had the towers removed and another story added. Subsequently, the old palace suffered the fate of many aristocratic dwellings. In 1895, it would house the offices of the Prague municipality. And only recently, since its restoration for official use by the Czech head of state, has Liechtenstein Palace regained some of its unmistakable elegance. Still, apart from the main portal, little remains to reflect the mansion's original Baroque glory.

opposite: *A view of the garden and the main entrance, which gives some sense of the palazzetto's unusual, hexagonal shape.*

Kaiserstein Palace

Franz Helfried, Baron von Kaiserstein, was one of those noblemen who could not be content with building just one palace. Four years after completing his summer residence on the banks of the Vltava (see Liechtenstein Palace), he commissioned what became a small masterpiece, erected below the Royal Palace on the east side of the Lesser Town Square (Malostranské náměstí). It would rise on the site of two houses inherited from his father-in-law, Jan de la Cron.

Despite its modest size, the mansion that Giovanni Baptista Alliprandi built in 1700–03 for Franz Helfried survives as one of his most impressive works. The elegant façade, marked by gray trim against a white ground, displays the imposing Kaiserstein arms above the balcony door on the piano nobile. Thanks to the tall windows, the architect achieved a suavely soaring effect despite the absence of other vertical features on the façade. The lower parts of the building, which cannot be seen from the square, are equally grand. Above meanwhile, there are the beautiful attic, with its consoles reminiscent of Palais Liechtenstein in Vienna, and the thrilling rooftop balustrade. Here the personifications of the Four Seasons, with their flowing draperies silhouetted against the sky, were created by the sculptor Ottavio Mosto. Originally, a pavilion with oval windows crowned the entire structure.

above: *The stucco-decorated ceiling, which dates from the 19th century.*

opposite: *The main façade with the Kaiserstein arms emblazoned above the balcony on the piano nobile. A ground-level loggia links the palace to the "U Splavinu" House next door.*

100

Sternberg Palace

Although invisible from Castle Square (Hradčanské náměstí), because situated on a low terrace above Stag Moat, Sternberg Palace is one of the finest examples of Baroque architecture from the turn of the 18th century. Its builder, Count Václav Adalbert von Sternberg, launched upon this town residence only after completing his lavish, costly villa in Troja. It was early in the 1690s that he began to acquire plots of land close by the Arch-bishop's Palace while also searching for an architect. Domenico Martinelli submitted plans in 1696, but a year later Count Sternberg chose a different proposal, which, however, included parts of Martinelli's design, essentially the rear section of the building. According to the latest information, it was Christoph Dientzenhofer who built and perhaps even designed the mansion, while Giovanni Baptista Alliprandi, named as the architect in earlier literature, worked on the project around 1706. However, by the time Count Sternberg died in 1708, his quadrangular palace had been completed, all but the front section, which would have reached up to Castle Square but remained unbuilt.

The entrance is difficult to find, being situated along a narrow alley leading away from the square. This makes the spacious vestibule and open stairway inside, the earliest of their kind in Prague, all the more a surprise for first-time visitors. Hidden away in the corners of the courtyard are other stairways, these marked by oval windows. The Sternbergs had

above: *The inner courtyard and the windows of one of the corner stairways.*

opposite: *Antoine-Louis Barye,* Lion Killing a Snake, *a 19th-century sculpture positioned near the entrance to the National Gallery's collection of modern French art.*

their reception rooms or piano nobile on the second story above the ground floor, where the windows are embellished with stucco shells and the keystones with medallion portraits of Roman Emperors. The exterior façade on the west swells at the center into a drum- or apse-like pavilion with a *sala terrena* that opens onto the beautiful garden.

Most of the wall paintings executed for Sternberg Palace are on the piano nobile, which does not include a grand hall or ballroom. The Countess's two sitting rooms contain a pair of paintings executed by Michael Václav Halbax on antique subjects: the suicide of Dido and the grieving Artemis, which together allegorize marital and extramarital love. The Classical and Chinese cabinets have paintings by Jan Rudolf Bys and stucco work by Giuseppe Donato Frisoni. Together they constitute heraldic allegories in a chiaroscuro or black-and-gold effect altogether rare in Prague. In the Chinese cabinet, Jan Václav Kratochvíl lacquered the walls in an East Asian manner.

Beginning in 1796, several members of the Sternberg family gave substantial support to the newly founded Society of Patriotic Art Lovers, an organization which they finally allowed to buy their estate at a very favorable price. Sternberg Palace thereupon became a venue for the first National Gallery of Prague, where the collection remained until 1871. The mansion then received the Institute for the Mentally Handicapped, as well as a military command. After World War II it again assumed the role of art gallery, where the National Gallery exhibits its collections of European art.

*A majolica relief by
Luca della Robbia, hung
in the main stairway
of Sternberg Palace.*

*Ceiling frescoes on
the piano nobile by
Michael Václav Halbax
(The Suicide of Dido)
and Matthias Nettel.*

*The beautiful stucco work
on these ceilings was executed
in the 18th century by
Giuseppe Donato Frisoni.
The salons would eventually become
a venue for Prague's National Gallery
at the time of it's inauguration
in the early 19th century.*

*View of the roof over
Sternberg Palace with
the oval pavilion beyond.*

107

Lobkovicz Palace

A number of Prague's palaces came into being at the behest of ambitious aristocrats eager to demonstrate their success through opulent and costly residences. One such dauntless spendthrift was Franz Karl, Count Přehořovsky von Kvasejovitz, a member of the Bohemian Vladyk family and the kind of man who prospered by making cash loans to the Treasury with funds borrowed on his own account. As a consequence, Count Přehořovsky rose to positions of power, becoming, among other things, President of the High Court as well as of the Court of Appeals. Eventually, however, his financial sleight of hand and the hard reality of his building expenditures combined to bankrupt him in 1714. Nonetheless, by this time he had already commissioned and constructed one of the masterpieces of European palace architecture.

Erected in 1703–07, the building now known as Lobkovicz Palace includes the advantages of an urban mansion along with those of a summer house. Situated in the small square at the top of the Vlasská, the building boasts a high façade with an enormous, two-story portal. The tall piano nobile and the drum-like central pavilion crowned by an attic balustrade with urns endow this side of the dwelling with a majestic appearance. The main façade, however, overlooks the gardens, where the central pavilion flanked by coved or curving wings, the garden walls, and the pergolas form an impressive architectural ensemble. This masterwork was created by Giovanni Baptista Alliprandi, a connoisseur of Viennese architecture, especially the buildings of Domenico Martinelli. The "abduction" sculptures atop the two gateposts probably originated in the studio of Lorenzo Mattielli in Vienna. The terraced gardens, designed in 1703 by the landscape gardener J.J. Kapula, became one of the famous sights of 18th-century Prague. In 1790 they were modified into an English park with the first *alpinum* in Bohemia.

The stuccos of Tommasso Soldati on the vestibule vault provide the framework for the frescoes of Johann Steinfels, who also painted the ceiling over the stairway. Here Mars and Bellona reign over an unrolled map of the palace, signifying that only peace makes possible the erection of architecture. The paintings date from the tenure of Count Franz Karl von Kolowrat-Liebsteinsky, who acquired the property in 1717. After 1753 the mansion belonged to the junior line of the princely Lobkovicz family. In 1769 Count August Anton von Lobkovicz added one story to each of the side wings.

*The Baroque staircase
recalls palaces in Vienna
designed by Domenico Martinelli.*

*The reception rooms of
the German Embassy, which now
occupies Lobkovicz Palace.*

*The best view of Lobkovicz Palace
is from the garden, where the the gate
is embellished with figure sculptures
by Lorenzo Mattielli.*

Since 1945 Lobkovicz Palace has been an embassy building, today occupied by the diplomatic mission from Germany. On the ground floor of the right wing, the library can still be admired for the snowy stucco work on its vaulted ceiling, which is painted with metamorphic scenes and garden views on a background of pink and green. The well-restored gardens also merit a long visit.

Far more interesting than
the majestic street façade
of Giovanni Baptista Alliprandi's
Lobkovicz Palace is the garden front.
Here the central, drum-like pavilion
crowned by an attic balustrade
with urns forms part of
a graceful ensemble that includes
concave or countercurving lateral wings,

all overlooking a garden studded
with pergolas and surrounded by
stone walls. The two posts on
either side of the gate leading to
and from the garden conclude in
tall "abduction" sculptures thought
to have originated in the studio
of Vienna's Lorenzo Mattielli.

Morzin Palace

Visitors ascending narrow Neruda Street (Nerudova), leading from the Lesser Town Square to Hradčany, soon find themselves confronted on the left by two gigantic Moors. With their steady gaze, massive musculature, and thick curls, their swollen cheeks and lips, the figures give the impression of being possessed of concentrated, resolute strength and power.

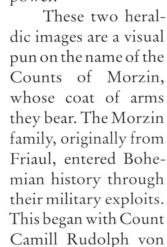

These two heraldic images are a visual pun on the name of the Counts of Morzin, whose coat of arms they bear. The Morzin family, originally from Friaul, entered Bohemian history through their military exploits. This began with Count Camill Rudolph von Morzin, who served as Colonel in the Imperial Cavalry during the Thirty Years War. Meanwhile, the builder of the palace served under Prince Eugene of Savoy, the savior of Vienna in the struggle against the Ottoman Turks.

In Morzin Palace the architect Giovanni Santini-Aichl produced one of his best works, as well as one of the finest examples of sculpture and architecture combined in harmonious interplay. Between 1713 and 1714 the architect succeeded in creating an extremely sophisticated street façade, perhaps because he lived directly opposite in Valkounsky House and could therefore observe the construction process daily and at close range. He insisted that the ground plan should follow that of four earlier houses on the site which had been integrated into one as early as 1670. The goal was achieved with elegance and at modest cost. The façade is quite simple, merely articulated by a series of Classical pilasters and a double molding, which does indeed seem to follow the old ground line quite closely, and a series of Classical pilasters. Statues representing the Four Parts of the World, executed by Ferdinand Maximilian Brokoff, parade across the attic. On either side of the central bay the two Moors serve as caryatids or atlantes supporting the balcony, while allegorical Night and Day figures stand guard at the main entrance.

The Morzin family having died out in the second half of the 19th century, their palace has housed the Romanian Embassy since the establishment of the first Czechoslovak Republic.

The main entrance to Morzin Palace (now the Romanian Embassy) with the allegorical bust Day.

112

opposite: *This gigantic Moor, one of two magnificent atlantes created by the sculptor Ferdinand Maximilian Brokof, constitutes a visual pun on the name of the Morzin family, who commissioned the architect Giovanni Santini-Aichl to build their palace in 1713-14.*

right and below: *Two salons in Morzin Palace, which today houses the Romanian Embassy. In the 18th century the rooms would have resounded to the music of Franz Joseph Haydn, who served the Morzin family as Kapellmeister at one of their country estates.*

115

Clam-Gallas Palace

When the Kinsky family built themselves a grand house in 16th-century Prague, it was on a site once occupied by several 12th- and 13th-century town houses and then by the domicile of Moravian Margrave John Henry, a brother of Charles IV. In 1634, following the disgrace and murder of Count Wilhelm Kinsky and Waldstein (Wallenstein) in Eger (Cheb), the Emperor Ferdinand II gave the confiscated Kinsky mansion to Matthias Gallas de Campo, the "iron" General of the Habsburgs' Imperial Army. The new owner's grandson, Count Jan Václav von Gallas, decided to exchange the rigors of military life for the refinements of diplomacy, which in turn required that he build an elegant residence commensurate with his several titles: Lord Marshall of the Kingdom of Bohemia, Administrator of the Duchy of Limburg, Imperial Ambassador in London and Rome, and finally Viceroy of Naples. In keeping with his ambition, Count Gallas acquired several neighboring houses, as well as the house on the corner of Mariánské náměstí that his father, Franz Ferdinand, had converted in 1685–93. All these additional properties permitted the old palace to be enlarged by a new wing, created in 1699–1700.

Even so, the expanded mansion proved too cramped and insufficiently grand to satisfy the needs of the owners demanding *train de vie*. Count Gallas therefore commissioned Johann Bernard Fischer von Erlach, the great Viennese court architect, to design

The public façade of Clam-Gallas Palace, designed to look onto a new square, which was never built, has had to content itself with narrow Husova Street. Still, the mansion remains one of the most beautiful aristocratic residences ever constructed in Prague.

opposite: *Matthias Bernhard Braun's muscle-flexing Titans welcome visitors at the main portal to Clam-Gallas Palace.*

a residence in the manner of Prince Eugene of Savoy's Winter Palais in Vienna. The solution Fischer devised for the Gallas problem can still be admired in Husova Street. Built in 1713–19, the new palace is quite simply one of the loveliest Baroque buildings in Europe. The generously proportioned structure has a fairly flat façade, even though endowed with well-articulated vertical axes, a tall central bay crowned by a wide triangular pediment, and projecting lateral pavilions with entrance portals below and balconies above. The sculptor Matthias Bernhard Braun created massive atlantes for the portals and a number of allegorical figures for the attic. All this magnificence derived in part from the architects assumption that the façade would be seen and admired from a certain distance. For this Count Gallas had planned to purchase the entire block of houses in front of his palace and there create a new square in the Old Town. Because the removal of tax-paying properties would have cost the Treasury considerable revenue, the Town Council denied the permission necessary for the new square to be installed.

This left the builder and his heirs free to concentrate more on the interior, beginning with the monumental stairway created under Count Philipp Joseph von Gallas, the son of the much-titled Jan Václav. The structure he oversaw is the most beautiful thing of its kind in all of Prague. Overhead

glows a trompe-l'oeil ceiling fresco – *The Triumph of Apollo* – by Carlo Innocenzo Carlone, who executed additional paintings of considerable interest in rooms on the floor above the piano nobile. The staircase is also peopled by statues from the workshop of Matthias Bernhard Braun, who went on to produce the Neptune Fountain in the first courtyard.

Count Philipp Joseph died in 1757, leaving the estate to his wife's nephew, Baron von Clam. At the end of the 18th century, the Clam-Gallas Counts presided over a cultural salon in their Prague mansion at which Mozart and Beethoven were both guests and performers. The years 1812–28 saw plays produced

opposite: *The grand staircase in Clam-Gallas Palace is decorated with putti, lanterns, and vases from the workshop of Matthias Bernhard Braun.*

As early as 1715 the Gallas Palace was generally praised as one of the most beautiful mansions in Prague.

left: *Carlo Innocenzo Carlone's* The Triumph of Apollo *glorifies the ceiling of the grand staircase in Clam-Gallas Palace.*

in the palace, which had the best private theater in Prague. During the 1860s the family had the inner rooms redecorated in the Neo-Rococo style.

After the destruction of the archive rooms in the Old Town Hall, during the Prague uprising of 1945, the authorities moved the city's valuable collection of archives into Clam-Gallas Palace, where the treasures have been exhibited on a number of occasions. The great house is now being restored, all the while that discussions continue concerning the role this jewel of the Viennese High Baroque should play in the cultural life of Prague.

Schönborn Palace

The growth of Prague's Lesser Town during the reign of Rudolph II produced an increasing demand for building sites, which in turn caused several of the gardens below Petřín Hill to be divided up after 1597. On one of the large sites, in what is now Market Street (Tržiště), the rich merchant Lazarus Henckel von Donnersmarck commissioned a grand Palladian residence designed by Giovanni Maria Filippi.

By the end of the Thirty Years' War, the mansion belonged to Count Rudolph von Colloredo-Wallsee, who, as Commander in Chief of Prague, had distinguished himself in the defense of the city against the Swedish Army. Prior of the Maltese Knights as well as a great military man, Count Rudolph had a rather modest palace erected on a site formerly occupied by five houses (including the Henckel mansion) and a vineyard. The long façade reflects the rhythm of the buildings it replaced. The main decorative feature is the embossed portal fitted with a well-preserved carved door from the Early Baroque period. The façade became more grand and ornate once Count Hieronymus von Colloredo had the architect Giovanni Baptista Alliprandi rebuild it in 1715–18.

The gardens merit far more attention than the palace, counting as they do among the most stylistically perfect of all Renaissance gardens. The terraces, sculptures, fountains, and gloriette, the latter converted from a wine press and placed on high ground, became one of the sights of Prague soon after the end of the Thirty Years' War. The renovations ordered by Count Colloredo endowed the palace with a more monumental garden entrance, including a new front wall and a stairway. The revised vestibule opens onto the gardens through a portal flanked by a pair of atlantes, thereby creating still greater contrast between the plain exterior and the ceremonial garden entrance.

In 1794 the palace devolved upon Count Hugo Damian von Schönborn, the progenitor of all three current lines of this Franconian family. The United States Embassy has long occupied Schönborn Palace, where the American flag, fluttering high above the garden pavilion, gave hope to the local population throughout the forty years of Communist rule.

below: *Today Schönborn Palace houses the Embassy of the United States of America.*

opposite: *The palace balcony overlooking the gardens offers a magnificent view towards Hradčany and the Lesser Town.*

Thun Palace

This palace, one of many in Prague bearing the name of the Thun family, can be found immediately below the rampart gardens on the steep slope of the southern terrace of Prague Castle. At the beginning of the 17th century it was the residence of Ferdinand Hoffmann von Grünbühel und Strechau, President of the Royal Treasury and one of the great patrons of both art and science during the reign of Rudolph II. The building's polygonal tower survives today. In 1634 the palace was acquired by Count Walter Leslie, a Cavalry Major who had become a protagonist in the Waldstein tragedy. This owner then sold the property to Count Guidobald von Thun, Archbishop of Salzburg, who refurbished it in the Early Baroque manner, an undertaking that began in 1659.

In the early 18th century, Thun Palace came in for a number of radical changes. From 1716 to 1727 the builder Jakob Achtzinger and the architect Giovanni Antonio Lurago erected the southwest wing. Working from a plan no longer known, they produced a splendid structure with two stories in back and four in front, the third one of which is gabled. Behind the palace, Count Oswald von Thun und Hohenstein (from the Klásterec nad Ohrí family) had terraced gardens laid out, showing just how durable this kind landscaping was. Although not very up to date, a terraced garden proved well suited to Prague.

overleaf: *Thun Palace is best seen from
its terraced gardens. The polygonal tower
survives from an earlier structure,
the 17th-century Hoffmann Palace.*

left: *Thun Palace seen
from the narrow Thunovská.*

In 1850 Bernard Grueber built a high Neo-Gothic gateway, which all but transformed the Thun residence into a secret, hidden palace. Eventually the Tudor Gothic structure proved its relevance when the British Embassy took over the property. Moreover, the palace remains in obscurity only from Thun Street (Thunovská). From the neighboring Hartig Garden, the mansion and its garden can be seen in all their beauty and charm.

126

Kolowrat-Thun Palace

Prague reveals one of its finest pieces of High Baroque palace architecture in the street façade of a unique complex situated near the Castle Steps (Zámecké schody). Behind the façade, the rear part of the ensemble derives from an elegant Renaissance palace of the Lords of Neuhaus, while the central section dates from 1672–78, when Johann Joachim von Slavata had it erected in the Early Baroque style. However, this same builder did not stop there, since the palace's monumental façade, with its giant pilasters, wealth of stucco work, and central stair tower, failed to have all the desired impact. To make it more conspicuous, Johann Joachim began buying up the adjacent town houses that cut off the main access to the palace from the road. Alas, he did not have enough time to complete the program.

This challenge remained for the Counts von Kolowrat-Liebsteinsky, the most powerful line of the many-branched Kolowrat family, whose seat was in Rychnov (Reichenau) in eastern Bohemia. Count Norbert Leopold, a passionate builder who played a major role in the erection of the nearby Church of St. Nicholas, made a start when he had Domenico Martinelli draw up plans, which unfortunately remained just that. However, his son, Count Norbert Vinzenz – a famously fat man whose boots the King of Poland kept in his cabinet of curiosities – proved intrepid enough to authorize construction, despite financial difficulties. The designer he chose

The main façade on Nerudova with the enormous eagles by Matthias Bernard Braun on either side of the central portal.

right: *In the 19th century the interior was converted to serve as the Prague headquarters of the Minister for Culture and Education, Count Franz von Thun-Hohenstein.*

below: *Restyled in the 19th century in the Neo-Rococo manner, these aristocratic rooms provided the setting for Count Franz von Thun's famous Saturday morning salons. Today they serve a similar purpose, but on behalf of the Italian Embassy, which now occupies the whole of Kolowrat-Thun Palace.*

opposite: *In the 19th century, the staircase in Kolowrat-Thun Palace was built in the Neo-Renaissance style by Josef Zítek.*

was his next-door neighbor, Giovanni Santini-Aichl, who thereupon produced his very best piece of palace architecture, comparable in quality to Palais Batthyány in Vienna. It would make the perfect setting for the large Kolowrat art collection (now in Rychnov). From this campaign came the wonderful façade with its two mighty eagles – the emblem of the Kolowrat Counts. A masterpiece by the sculptor Matthias Bernard Braun, the great birds perch daringly on tiny rocks while spreading their vast wings to support figures of Juno and Jupiter seated upon two enormous volutes. Flanking the impressive entrance to the vestibule are a pair of oval windows so characteristic of Santini as to be virtual signatures.

In 1768 the palace passed through marriage to the Counts von Thun und Hohenstein, who would play an important role in the history of 19th-century Bohemia. During the 1840s, Count Franz von Thun, the future Minister for Culture and Education, made the great mansion the scene of his famous Saturday morning salons, attended by a select group of artists, especially painters. His successor, Count Friedrich von Thun, turned the family palace into a political club for the conservative nobility. The Thuns also left their mark on the interior by restyling it, especially the monumental stair hall, which was rebuilt by Josef Zítek, the designer of the Prague National Theater, and decorated with frescoes by Frantisek Zenísek, Joseph Scheiwl, and Josef Tulka allegorizing the life of man from cradle to grave.

The Italian Embassy now occupies the entire complex of Kolowrat-Thun Palace.

Villa Amerika

In the side streets of the upper New Town glitters a small Baroque jewel set like an oasis at the center a utilitarian hospital district full of clinics and blocks of flats. Jan Václav, Count Michna, had it erected in 1717-20 as a small temple of the muses, designed by Kilian Ignaz Dientzenhofer, who went on to become the most celebrated member of a family of builders active throughout Franconia and Bohemia. At the time of his work for Count Michna, young Dientzenhofer was at the beginning of a career, with his energies devoted mainly to churches. Even so, the little summer palace is a fully seasoned example of small-scale, beautifully balanced architecture, which here consists of a two-story central building with a mansard roof and two small outbuildings on either side of the main gate. The ensemble radiates charm, thanks not only to the shape of the main structure, which is unique to Prague, but also the décor, the reduced scale of all the forms, and, of course, the garden. Also contributing to the sense of enchantment are the paintings and garden sculptures, especially the wrestling Giants and the Four Seasons by Matthias Bernhard Braun. Within the villa are frescoes by Jan Ferdinand Schor depicting Apollo scattering the muses' gifts of flowers among putti, as well as illusionistic representations of the Greco-Roman deities.

The first threat to the summer house came at the end of the 18th century, which saw cattle markets held in the garden. A century later the villa once again

Matthias Bernhard Braun's Autumn, *one of the allegorical Four Seasons made for the garden of Villa Amerika.*

opposite: The 18th-century villa within the intimacy of its setting, which includes not only a delightful garden but also a pair of small outbuildings on either side of the entrance gate.

At the end of the 19th century,
the beautiful gardens of Count Michna
were tuned into a stockyard,
where the animals wandered among
Braun's magnificent sculptures.
Fortunately, Villa Amerika has been
the home of the arts since 1932, when
it became the Antonín Dvořák Museum.

barely escaped destruction when the new medical school moved in. Fortunately, the building survived its occupation by science and returned to the fine arts in 1932. Now the villa became the home of the Antonín Dvořák Museum, and today, more than ever, music fills the great Baroque hall. Even though Dvořák lived in the United States for several years, the name "Amerika" has nothing to do with his career. Rather it arrived in the second half of the 19th century for reasons no longer remembered.

above: *The main façade of Count Michna's pleasure pavilion.*

left: *A detail of the grille that crowns the main gate to Villa Amerika and its garden.*

opposite: *In the Villa Amerika garden,* Wrestling Giant *by Matthias Bernard Braun.*

*Today Villa Amerika houses a museum
dedicated to the Czech composer Antonín Dvořák.
Thus, music is still played at Villa Amerika,
built in the 18th century as a "Temple of the Muses".*

*Villa Amerika, the most delicious bit of Rococo
architecture in Prague, was designed by Kilian Ignaz
Dientzenhofer at the very beginning of what would
evolve into an exceptionally distinguished career.
In this joyous, youthfil enclave, the Muses appear truly
to have sung into a fine-tuned and sensitive ear.*

*Trompe-l'oeil painting – representing
sculptures and architecture as well as
sky effects – by Jan Ferdinand Schor decorates
the rooms within Villa Amerika, a name of
unknown origin having nothing to do with
Antonín Dvořák's career in the United States.*

Kaunitz Palace

Beginning with the Early Baroque period, the New Town, which was less built up, gained favor among the nobility as a place for erecting their new urban residences, especially since the area offered room for gardens. Here, in 1663, the Silesian Baron Johann Ernst Schaffgotsch bought a plot of land in Panská Street. In 1725 his nephew, Count Johann Anton Schaffgotsch, the Supreme Burgrave of Bohemia, replaced the original house built there with a completely new palace, its main entrance accented by a huge portal with a broken pediment and a pair of showy volutes. The architect remains unknown, although it has been suggested that Giovanni Baptista Alliprandi and Franz Maximilian Kaňka may have been involved.

In 1782 Count Philipp Joseph Kinsky bought the property and had it expanded by two pavilion wings and the interior redesigned in a Classicizing manner by Matthias Hummel. It was here that, following the Battle of Aspern in 1809, Count Kinsky gave refuge to Archduke Charles. The next owner, Count Hugo Karl von Salm-Reifferscheid, a Moravian aristocrat and the owner of ironworks, left his mark on the palace when he had the main hall embellished with stuccos in the Neo-Rococo manner and beautiful romantic wall paintings devoted to Old German motifs. These were selected from the Nibelungenlied and the troubadour poems of Hartmann von Aue and Wolfram von Eschenbach.

above: *The main hall with its program of fresco decorations derived from Old German myths. Commissioned by Count Hugo Karl von Salm-Reifferscheid, the date from the early 19th century and reflect the Romantic spirit of that time.*

opposite: *The main façade of Kaunitz Palace, with its huge windows on the piano nobile, faces Mostecká Street.*

139

Mladota Palace

One of the most familiar legends of Prague hovers about Mladota Palace, which occupies the southwest corner of Charles Square (Karlovo náměstí), once the site of the cattle market in New Town. Here as well, the legend tells us, stood the house in which the highly cultivated Dr. Faustus practiced alchemy, acquiring immense wealth and great knowledge thanks to his pact with the Devil. One day, the Devil claimed his due and carried the Doctor off to Hell, straight through the ceiling of the laboratory, which left a hole that could never be repaired. The tale is traditionally told with lavish detail, as well as in a number of variants and even with sequels. It is of course the local Prague version of the famous German Renaissance story of Faust.

However mythic the Faust legend, there is no question that the palace seen here has connections with alchemy and the natural sciences. During the reign of Charles IV, the Troppau Dukes maintained their residence on a site once occupied by the palaces of the Mladota family of Solopisk. The Troppaus' Gothic mansion burned down in 1434, to be replaced by a town house for Prokop, the New Town chronicler and city scribe. Already letters from the period speak of the house in relation to alchemy. In 1543 Johann Kopp von Raumenthal, King Ferdinand's physician and the author of widely read medical books, acquired the property. Later,

Joachim Ulrich von Neuhaus, the Lord Chancellor of Bohemia, stayed there during his visits to Prague. By 1606, Martin Karban of Olsany had converted the building into a mansion with a corner tower. Shortly afterwards, Edward Kelley, Rudolph II's famous and adventurous alchemist, moved in.

In 1724 the dwelling came into the possession of Ferdinand Anton, Baron Mladota of Solopisk, a dilettante chemist, who enjoyed showing his experiments to friends. It was at this time that the Renaissance building underwent refurbishment in the Baroque style. Seriously damaged during the Seven Years' War, the palace was once again renovated, this time in the Rococo manner, a task carried out by the architect Joseph Jèger, working for the administrator of the nearby Church of St. John of the Rock (linked to the house by a fine Baroque garden wall). Mladota Palace survives in that form, but as part of the building complex of the Prague General Hospital.

opposite above: The pedimented gable of Mladota Palace looming behind the monument to Svatopluk Presl, a 19th-century Czech botanist.

opposite below: The main façade of the Baroque mansion popularly known as "Faust House", once the residence of Edward Kelley, Emperor Rudolph II's famous alchemist.

Palace of the Grand Priory

Sovereign Order of the
Knights of Malta

The first order of knights – the Knights of St. John of Jerusalem – came to Bohemia under Vladislav II. Only recently has it been discovered that the Maltese Knights or Knights of Malta – as the Knights of St. John were later called after their seat on the island of Malta – began to build their Prague priory in 1169. The Order controlled a generous amount of land around the Church of St. Mary, at a strategic position next to the Lesser Town side of the bridge. As a result, the Church of St. Mary of the Knights of St. John was called St. Mary at the Bridgehead. Only later would it be called St. Mary beneath the Chain, presumably for the chain around the area dominated by the Order, which eventually became a separate enclave with its own defensive fortification, and it would remain a self-sufficient administrative and jurisdictional entity until the end of the 18th century.

The Hussite Wars of 1419–35 did considerable damage to the Grand Priory in Prague, after which the building would not be renovated until the early 17th century, a campaign carried out by Prior Matthèus Dippold von Lobkovicz. But instead of restoring the church to its original length, Prior Matthèus had a Late Renaissance building erected on the east, in place of a hospital, as the Grand Prior's own residence. Still, the renovation continued right up to the end of the Thirty Years' War, when the head of the Maltese Order was Count Rudolph von Colloredo-Wallsee, one of Prague's most successful defenders against the Swedish invasion of 1648. In the church he is represented by a white marble statue dating from the mid-19th century. In 1650 the high altar gained a new painting – *The Battle of Lepanto* – executed by the Czech artist Karel Skréta, who also painted the portrait of Bernard de Witte, the very active Prior of Colloredo.

Not until the early 18th century did any new building take place in the Grand Priory. Finally, in 1726, construction began on a new palace, designed by the Italian architect Bartolomeo Scotti from Valle d'Intelvi. Hard by the massive, twin-spired Gothic church Scotti erected a pleasant two-wing mansion that was more intimate than remarkable or spacious. It would be completed under Grand Prior Prince Gundakar Poppo von Dietrichstein, whose coat of arms endows a very sober façade with its most impressive decoration. On one side the palace faces the square in front of the church (main entrance), while the other side looks onto Grand Priory Square (Velkopřevorské náměstí) towards Buquoy Palace. Large vases by the sculptor Matthias Bernard Braun surmount the two portals, rising halfway up the wall of the piano nobile. The same artist also created the torchbearer figures in the elegant stairway on the interior. Here, the most splendid room is the main hall, but, apart from the stuccos, all that remains of its former glory is a tall gilt stove set into one wall. Originally, the most imposing decoration was a Brussels tapestry made especially for the room by Peter von der Hecke, but removed during World War II.

*The Palace of
the Grand Priory
of the Knights of Malta
seen from the front.*

*The interior of St. Mary
beneath the Chain, a church
mentioned as early the 12th century.
The painting above the altar,*
The Battle of Lepanto *by Karel Skréta,
dates from the mid-17th century.*

*The palace of the Grand Priory,
built in 1726, juxtaposed to
the much older church of St. Mary,
both seen from the garden.*

In 1952 the Palace of the Grand Priory became the home of the cellection of antique musical instruments formerly housed at the National Museum in Prague. More than thirty-five years later, in 1989, the sovereign Order of Malta regained control of its palace in Prague. By this time the mansion had fallen into deep dilapidation, a situation that Max Turnauer, ambassador from the Maltese Order, set about to reverse. Only recently has this program succeeded in restoring the property to its original beauty.

144

*A large reception room
in the Palace of the Grand Priory
of the Knights of Malta.*

146

*In this comfortable modern salon
in the Palace of the Grand Priory,
all that remains of former splendor
is the gilded ceramic heating stove.*

147

The armorial bearings high
on the wall of the grand staircase
are those of former Priors of
the Order of the Knights of Malta.

opposite: The "Maltese Palace"
boasts one of the grandest staircases
in Prague, a masterwork embellished
with sculptures by the celebrated
artist Matthias Bernard Brown.

Colloredo-Mansfeld Palace

The old mansion formerly on the site of Colloredo-Mansfeld Palace belonged to, among others, Count Joachim Andreas Schlick, a leading figure in the Bohemian uprising of 1618–20. The night following the ill-fated Battle of the White Mountain, the unfortunate old Count opened his house on Charles Street (Karlova) to the "Winter King," Frederick of the Palatinate. Having joined the losing party, he would die on the gallows in the Old Town Square (Staroměstské náměstí).

Colloredo-Mansfeld Palace, built in the early 1730s for Count Vincez Paul von Mansfeld-Fondi, would have a quite different fate, thanks in part to the enlightened reign of the Empress/Queen Maria Theresia. Behind Franz Ignaz Prée's flat façade, decorated as well as articulated by a wealth of stucco work, a rich and varied cultural life unfolded. It found its focal point in the large oval hall, under a ceiling covered with a vast and dramatic fresco entitled *The Gathering of the Gods on Olympus*. Painted by Giovanni Pietro Scotti of Bologna, a collaborator of Carlo Carlone, it dates from 1736. Although the design and even some details of the hall derive from models in both Prague and Vienna, the result is one of the loveliest interiors in the Bohemian capital. The sculptural ornaments came from the workshop of Anton Braun, who in the 1730s carved the putti-embellished coat of arms as well as the Triton fountain (later crudely restored).

The lively cultural tradition that began under Maria Theresia – for which one has only to think of the picture collection still housed in Opočno Palace – continued to flourish in the 19th century. In 1840, the Bohemian Art Association held its first public exhibition at Colloredo-Mansfeld Palace, a show that included works by foreign as well as Czech artists.

above: *The watercolor dates from around 1840 and represents a small drawing room used by Countess Colloredo in that period.*

opposite: *The main entrance to Colloredo-Mansfeld Palace on Charles Street (Karlova), its portal partly concealed by the portico of the Church of St. Savior.*

151

above: *The ceiling over the great oval hall in Colloredo-Mansfeld Palace dissolves in the illusionism of Giovanni Pietro Scotti's fresco.*

opposite: *The cornice in the great oval hall is supported by massive voluted consoles and embellished with freestanding figures executed in the 1730s by an unknown sculptor.*

Buquoy Palace

I n a quiet corner of the Lesser Town, at 9 Grand Priory Square (Velkopřevorské náměstí), an elegant late Baroque Palace hides behind a sheltering grove of magnificent chestnut trees. Today it houses the French Embassy.

The first Buquoy to settle in Bohemia, from the family seat in Brabant, was Charles Bonaventura de

Longueval, Baron de Vaux, Comte de Buquoy, and Imperial Commander at the Battle of the White Mountain in 1620. By acquiring the mansion in Grand Priory Square in 1748, the Buquoys gained a residence worthy of their status as large landowners in southern Bohemia.

By this time the palace had been completed; otherwise, the architectural history of the house is not yet entirely clear. Research suggests that in the years 1675–94 the Archbishop of Prague, Count Johann Friedrich von Waldstein, owned a fine residence on the site, an edifice with two tower-like pavilions presumably commissioned by the Archbishop himself and possibly designed by Jean-Baptiste Mathey. The palace would have formed the core of the present one, which was most likely constructed after 1736 and then bought by Countess Marie Anna Hrzán von Harras. The new owner had the Waldstein dwelling renovated, along with the seminary of the Knights of Malta and the so-called Little Buquoy Palace. The architect in charge was Johann Georg Aichbauer, stepbrother of Kilian Ignaz Dientzenhofer.

The Late Baroque main façade of Buquoy Palace rises behind a splendid grove of chestnut trees in idyllic Grand Priory Square.

The grand stairway in Buquoy Palace leads to the reception rooms of the French Ambassador.

The inner courtyard of Buquoy Palace.

After 1860 the interior underwent refurbishment in the Neo-Baroque style, while the exterior retained its original Baroque character. The flat façade culminates in a wide triangular pediment spread over the central bays. In front of two impressive, heavily voluted portals stands a row of well-preserved hitching posts, a survival from the past that contributes to the intimate atmosphere of Grand Priory Square.

The more intimate rooms within Buquoy Palace, such as the bedroom and its anteroom, have gained comfort without sacrificing their style.

In Buquoy Palace the French Embassy
has embellished its reception rooms
with exquisite paintings and furniture.
The valuable tile stoves date
from renovations effected in the 1860s.

161

*Neo-Baroque prevails even
in the private apartments
of the French Ambassador
in Buquoy Palace.*

*The full-length portrait
above the canapé in the antechamber
represents the Duc d'Abrantès,
clad in the uniform of
a General in the French Army.*

Sylva-Taroucca Palace

This Late Baroque palace, situated on the moat (Na Příkopě) in the New Town, was commissioned by Prince Ottavio Picco-lomini, scion of a Sienese family prominent in the military life of Austria during the 17th and 18th centuries. Indeed, Prince Ottavio, who died in 1757,

held the post of Imperial Generalis-simo when he undertook to build the family palace in Prague. Even after having accepted the plans drawn up by Milanese architect Carlo Giuseppe Merlo, Prince Ottavio finally assigned the project to Kilian Ignaz Dientzenhofer. A Classical, rational structure erected in 1744–52, the palace comprises a rusticated ground floor, a piano nobile with eight bays marked off by tall, flat pilasters, and a brief attic crowned by a broad triangular pediment at the center and two smaller segmental pediments on either side. From one of the liveliest streets in Prague, the palace extends deep into the site, where its two courtyards with their beautiful fountains evoke, even today, the celebratory atmosphere of the Baroque Age. Behind the palace there originally stood a riding school, but neither it nor the surrounding garden has survived.

Within the great house, a colonnaded vestibule leads to an imposing staircase designed by Anselmo Lurago, who completed Dientzenhofer's work. The esoterically balanced stucco decorations of Carlo Giuseppe Bossi, Ignác Platzer's sculptures of playful putti, and ornamental grillework breathe the spirit of

above: *Two of Ignác Platzer's playful putti decorating one of the loveliest stairways in Prague.*

opposite: *Václav Bernard Ambrozi's ceiling fresco,* Helios in His Chariot, *and sculptural personifications of the Seasons bring beauty and distinction to the grand staircase.*

the Rococo. Overhead Václav Bernard Ambrozi executed the illusionistic ceiling fresco with its conventional subject of Helios in his chariot.

Eventually the palace passed into the hands of the Sylva-Taroucca family from Portugal. Emmanuel Tellez da Sylva-Taroucca served Empress Maria Theresia so well that she made him a Duke. His

Within Sylva-Taroucca Palace, Ignác Platzer's Flora *dominates the wonderful staircase.*

descendants would emerge as prominent patrons of the arts in the 19th century. Count Ernest Emmanuel von Sylva-Taroucca, the last Imperial Minister of Agriculture and the instigator of the lovely park in Pruhonice near Prague, even opened his palace for an exhibition of ethnographic works in 1895–1903.

For almost a century, Sylva-Taroucca Palace has housed the historic Café Savarin, joined more recently by the Austrian Casino.

opposite: *Sylva-Taroucca Palace turns its broad Late Baroque façade and triple entrance towards the lively scene on Na Příkopě.*

The piano nobile within Sylva-Taroucca Palace is now used by the Austrian Casino.

Fürstenberg Palace

Fürstenberg Palace comes at the end of the palatial row along Valdštejnská. Unlike its neighbors, the mansion does not face the street but, rather, looks onto gardens spread out at the foot of the steep Castle Steps.

Until the mid-16th century, this part of the Lesser Town was given over to gardens and vineyards. However, once Rudolph II established his court in Prague, the quarter, like others on the periphery of the Lesser Town, witnessed an explosion of construction activity. One of the builders was Václav Berka von Dubá, from a leading Bohemian Catholic family, who had a Renaissance residence built for himself on several adjoining plots.

The palace aquired its present form during a renovation carried out in 1743-47 at the command of the recently ennobled Baron Václav Kazimir Netolocky von Eisenberg, the Lord Chief Justice of Bohemia. Behind the relatively plain façade of the quadrangular Late Baroque building glitters an extravagant interior. The most notable room is the main hall embellished with stuccos and a fresco devoted to the goddess Diana, the latter executed by an unknown master. In the 18th century the spacious room served as a theater.

In 1822 the palace came into the possession of Prince Karl Egon von Fürstenberg, a learned

aristocrat whose scientific collections and valuable library are now housed in Krivoklát Castle. The Fürstenbergs had iron foundries on their estates, and for a long time they used the gardens of Fürstenberg Palace to market their famous cast-iron work. The gardens would be restored at the end of the 19th century. Since 1935 the palace has been occupied by the Polish Embassy.

Fürstenberg Palace, the last in a row of mansions on Valdštejnská, faces away from the street towards the gardens below Pargue Castle. Thus, the garden entrance serves as the main entrance to the palace itself.

The ceiling of the great hall, which dates from the 18th century, is decorated with a fresco featuring the goddess Diana.

Goltz-Kinsky Palace

The east side of the Old Town Square is dominated by Goltz-Kinsky Palace, thanks to a façade projected far more aggressively into the public space than any other house in what is a very old former market site. No other structure either here or in the heart of the quarter can compare

with the bold conception of this palatial dwelling. The form and setting of the mansion derive from changes wrought during the High and Late Baroque periods. Until the end of the 17th century the façades of patrician houses, together with the Teyn School and the Town Hall, gave the square its overall character. Come the Baroque Age, however, magnificent churches and palaces replaced the more modest structures of earlier times.

Count Johann Ernst von der Goltz commissioned the present palace, a work designed probably by Kilian Ignaz Dientzenhofer shortly before his death. Between 1755 and 1765 Anselmo Lurago updated certain aspects of the original scheme and then erected a massive structure on the site of two medieval houses, decorating the façade with a wealth of stucco work. Ignác Platzer created the statuary on the attic as well as on the sloping sides of the two pediments.

Count von der Goltz died shortly after the building and decorative work had been completed. His window then sold the property for 35,000 gulden

to Count Franz Ulrich Kinsky, a Bohemian patriot was well as the Imperial Privy Councillor and Commander in Chief of the Artillery. In 1830 Prince Rudolph Kinsky had the interior renovated in the Classical style and the house expanded in the back. During this campaign the palace gained its grand staircase, a work designed by Jindrich Koch.

Goltz-Kinsky Palace has witnessed signal events in modern Czechoslovak history. On February 25, 1948, the date of the Communist takeover, Klement Gottwald, the party's leader, stepped onto the balcony and announced to the workers' militia that, despite the electoral results, President Edvard Beneš had succumbed to pressure and appointed a new government. With this, Czechoslovakia began four decades of Communist domination. On February 25, 1990, President Václav Havel stood on the same balcony and announced to the assembled people of Prague that democracy had returned to their country for good. Meanwhile, throughout the postwar era, the old palace has been the repository of the National Gallery's precious collection of graphic art, consisting of some 15,000 prints and drawings.

Goltz-Kinsky Palace, with its façade lavishly embellished with stucco reliefs, dominates the east side of the Old Town Square. The relief sculpture within the pediment on the right represents the centaur Nessus and the nymph Dejanira. The father of Franz Kafka had his shop behind the palaces ground-floor windows.

below: *This watercolor of 1935
re-creates the painting atelier of
Countess Kinsky in Goltz-Kinsky Palace*

bottom: *A watercolor of Prince Kinsky's
study as it was in 1840.*

right: *Goltz-Kinsky Palace is without
doubt the most beautiful Rococo mansion in Prague.*

176

*On the main façade of
Goltz-Kinsky Palace the subject
of relief in the left pediment
is the Rape of Europa.*

*The main wing of Goltz-Kinsky Palace
contains a magnificent staircase in
the Empire style. Today the reception rooms,
also Empire in style, house the National Gallery's
very important collections of prints and drawings.*

*Eighteenth-century
Goltz-Kinsky Palace,
with its Rococo dormers,
abuts a 16th-century
Late Gothic house known
as "At the Stone Bell"
(U kamenného zvonu).*

The Archbishop's Palace

In 1561, the Roman Catholic see of Prague gained an Archbishop for the first time in more than a century, following the conclusion of the Hussite Wars. The prelate – Anton Brus von Müglitz – installed himself in a Renaissance palace acquired for the purpose by Ferdinand I from the Griessbeck von Griessbach family, Bavarian aristocrats who had built their mansion adjacent the moat in Castle Square. Already in 1559, a chapel had been erected and its walls decorated with semifigurative stuccos representing persons important in Bohemian Church history. The frescoed ceiling radiated scenes devoted to the Holy Trinity and the Life of John the Baptist, all painted by the Prague master Daniel Alexius of Kvetná. Despite later rebuilding, the wonderful Renaissance structure has survived, thanks to the cautious Counter-Reformation program carried out by Archbishop Sbinko Berka von Dubá.

Bolder modifications, however, came during the Baroque period, when Count Johann Friedrich von Waldstein commissioned Jean-Baptiste Mathey, a French architect educated in Rome, to modernize the palace from top to bottom. What resulted was a monumental freestanding structure whose three stories crowned by a roof pavilion would dominate Castle Square. The marble portal created at this time still forms the main entrance to the building.

When, during the reign of Maria Theresia, the Royal Castle was renovated by Pacassi and the moat between the Castle and the Hradčany filled in, Archbishop Anton Count Příchovský responded in 1764 by having the Archepiscopal Palace transformed yet again. A demanding and cultivated aristocrat, Archbishop Příchovský commissioned the architect Johann Joseph Wirch to add two wings and reconstruct the façade in a lavish Rococo style, complete with an abundance of stucco work and figure sculptures from the workshop of Ignác Platzer. The grand reception rooms were hung with magnificent Gobelins tapestries, which together with the collection of art works, the priceless library, and, of course, the architecture made the Archbishop's Palace a mansion that contemporaries described in the most glowing terms.

Platzer's Giants, installed atop the gateposts leading into Prague Castle, contemplate the sun setting behind the façade of the Archbishops Palace.

The façade of the Archbishop's Palace,
rebuilt in an elegant Rococco manner by
Johann Joseph Wirch, stands guard over
Castle Square and the entrance to Prague Castle.
The sculptures atop the attic and the pedimented
roof pavilion were created by Ignác Platzer.

*The grand staircase leading
to the reception halls on
the piano nobile. The charm
of the putti torchbearers,
the graceful sweep of
the broad steps, and
the curvilinear elegance
of the openwork chandelier
and balustrades date from
the 18th century, when*

*Archbishop Anton Count Přichovsky
had the palace renovated
in a aristocratic Rococco style.*

183

left: *The gallery hung with portraits of Prague's Archbishops.*

below: *Another portrait gallery, this one devoted to Popes.*

opposite: *The frescoed chapel, which dates from 1599, is the only part of the original Renaissance/Mannerist building to survive in the palace of the Roman Catholic Archbishops of Prague. The niches contain busts of the prelates who took part in the synod of 1605.*

185

*One of the eight Gobelins tapestries
that decorate the upstairs reception rooms
un the Archbishop's Palace. Woven during
the 18th century, they came from
the Nielson atelier in Paris.*

186

*The tile stoves in
the partrician salons of
the Archbishop's Palace
date from the beginning
of the 18th century.
The paintings are portraits
of the Habsburg Emperors.*

Turba Palace

One of the most charming Rococo buildings in Prague is a small palace that stands on the west side of Maltese Square (Maltézské náměstí) not far from Nostitz Palace. It was erected in 1765–67, on the site of two burnt-out houses, for Francis Xavier von Turba, a Knight who also owned the neighboring Musconi House, so called for one of the richest Italian merchants in Prague during the reign of Rudolph II. The architect in charge of the playful mansion seen here was Joseph Jäger, a Tyrolean settled in the Lesser Town since 1753. This self-confident form-giver, who became court architect to the Elector of Bavaria in 1769, then proceeded to build his own house next door, doing so on a scale that somewhat overpowered Turba Palace.

A four-story structure, with its façade articulated by eight Ionic pilasters and two lateral round-headed pediments filled with exuberant Rococo ornamentation, evinces a whimsicality that makes it seem especially suitable for its current occupant – the Japanese Embassy – which has been in residence since 1924.

above: *This small palace fits quietly into the row of buildings on the west side of Maltese Square.*

188

*Rainy nights bring out
all the charm of the Lesser Town
lamps casting their light and reflections
on the granite paving stones of Prague.*

189

Pachta Palace

Just off Annen Square (Annenské náměstí) beyond a mask-embellished portal stands the smallest of the three palaces formerly owned in Prague by the Counts Pachta von Rayhofen. Here the comfort and idyllic atmosphere of the Rococo period survives in all their sweetness and delight. The present mansion replaced an earlier one in which Count Johann Joachim, to whom the Pachta family owed their reputation and wealth, was arrested and taken hostage in 1742 by the French military. Shortly afterwards he died in solitary confinement. His sons, who had successful careers of their own, consoled themselves by building three new palaces in Prague.

Count Hubert Karl Pachta built the palace situated between Annenské náměstí, Strbrná, Náprstkova, and Karoliny Světlé, the design for which he sought from Johann Joseph Wirch, an architect active in Prague during the third quarter of the 18th century. A quadrangular two-story structure erected around an intimate courtyard, the house boasts a balconied portico, a staircase decorated with putti from the workshop of Ignác Platzer, and façades plain enough to escape notice in the narrow lanes of Old Town. There was also a small garden along the river until the 1840s, when the palace lost its panoramic view over the Vltava to a block of flats. In the golden days of the late 18th century, Mozart and other leading musicians gave concerts here, for the Pachta von Rayhofen family loved art and maintained a celebrated orchestra of their own.

Even today peace reigns in this enchanted corner of Prague Old Town. It is sometimes discovered by those who attend performances at the neighboring Theater on the Balustrade (Divadlo na zábradlí), in whose courtyard they may also encounter the "playwright in residence" – Václav Havel.

below: *A view from the courtyard balcony.*

opposite: *The staircase with its figures from the atelier of Ignác Platzer.*

*At Pachta Palace, the slow,
graceful curves of the portico
reinforce the intimate character
of the interior courtyard.*

*Few palaces of Prague can boast
a more active or distinguished musical history
than Pachta palace. It was here, for instance,
that Count Johann Joachim Pachta induced Mozart
to compose a pair of dance pieces – by looking
the composer in his room! In 1787, after hearing
the six Contre-danses created by Mozart
during his stay in Pachta Palace, Bonini,
the Italian director of the Prague theater,
commissioned the Salzburg genius to
undertake the opera Don Giovanni, which had
its premiere at Prague later in the same year.*

*opposite: One of Ignác Platzer's
putti sculptures decorating the staircase
within Pachta Palace.*

Kolowrat Palace

On the right of Valdštejnská where the street narrows towards Waldstein Square (Valdštejnské náměstí) a long façade stretches out to follow the road as it makes a gentle curve. This is Kolowrat Palace, a seventeen-bay mansion that may constitute the last of the great aristocratic dwellings built in Prague during the Baroque era.

It was Countess Maria Barbara Czernín (née Countess Schaffgotsch) who had an older house on the site replaced with the present palace, a residence designed and built by Ignác Palliardi, who belonged to an Italian family long resident in Prague. Although working at a time when Neo-Classicism had already become the fashion, Palliardi delivered to his employer, no doubt at her request, a structure still fully immersed in the Rococo. This is most evident in the vivaciously elaborated façade, with its central pavilion crowned by a pediment set with an image of the Virgin Mary at the center of curvilinear stucco relief work.

To the left of Kolowrat Palace, beyond the "Little Czernín Palace," unfolds one of the loveliest terraced gardens in this part of town, a bit of landscaped nature laid out in 1769–89. Here the Rococo reigns supreme even more than in the mansion. The entrance is through a *glorietta,* from which the garden steps upwards along its main axis. The balustraded terraces overlook a small pool as well as

*The central pavilion of the main façade
of Kolowrat Palace emblazoned with the Kolowrat arms
and an image of the Virgin Mary at the center
of the wide pediment decorated with stucco reliefs
executed in the curvilinear Rococo manner.*

a *sala terrena* in the form of a delicate loggia bearing the Czernín and Schaffgotsch coat of arms. They also offer a pleasing view of the city.

In the course of the 19th century the palace changed hands several times, until 1867 when it came into the possession of Prince Friedrich Wilhelm of Hessen-Kassel und Hanau. Only in 1886 did the Kolowrat Counts assume ownership and renovate the interior in the Neo-Baroque style. Between the two World Wars the Czechoslovak government acquired Kolowrat Palace, which made it the scene of the unhappy events of 1938. Today the mansion houses the Czech Ministry of Culture.

The Neo-Baroque rooms and grand staircases
created in the late 19th century by the Counts von Kolowrat
now house he Czech Ministry of Culture.
Kolowrat Palace holds the distinction of being,
perhaps, the last of the great aristocratic dwellings
built in Prague during the Baroque era.

Young Richard Wagner, during
his first visit to Prague, fell in love
with not one but two daughters – Jenny and
Augusta – of the Kolowrat household.
Today Kolowrat Palace houses
the Czech Ministry of Culture.

It was in these elegant neo-Baroque
rooms that President Edvard Beneš struggled
to lead his nation during the critical days
of 1938, when the Western powers abandoned
Czechoslovakia to the aggressions of Nazi Germany,
whose occupation of the Sudetenland became the first act
in the unfolding tragedy of World War II.

199

Thun Palace

Home of the Bohemian Diet

Nothing survives of the palace that Jakob Achtzinger built in 1696-1720, from plans by an unknown architect, for Count Maximilian von Thun und Hohenstein in the Lesser Town. An engraving from the 1730s reveals the mansion to have been a large, stern, sober structure, whose interior found its chief decoration in a cycle of ceiling and wall frescoes executed in the great hall by the Austrian painter Johann Michael Rottmayr before 1700. Beginning in 1779 the theater company of Pasquale Bondini would perform here in rooms specially designed for that purpose. In the late 1780s Thun Palace became the setting for a casino that catered to the nobility. In 1794, however, a fire gutted the mansion, leaving the remains to be acquired by the Bohemian Estates, which in 1801 refashioned the property as the home of the Bohemian Diet. This was when the palace gained its simple, Classicized façade pierced by two widely set portals.

Thun Palace thus played a central role in the revival of parliamentary life in Bohemia. For almost two hundred years the Diet has traditionally met here, except during the most difficult periods of Czech history. One of these came during World War I, when the Supply Commission used the building as a grain depot, and another during World War II, when the German Army occupied Prague. Following the Communist putsch of February 1948 the Diet

above: *The long, Classicized street façade of Thun Palace, the traditional seat of the Bohemian the Diet.*

opposite: *Called* The Lion of Bohemia, *this modern sculpture stands before Thun Palace.*

again ceased to assemble. On November 14, 1918, the National Assembly declared that the House of Habsburg had lost the throne of Bohemia, whereupon the building became the seat of the Senate.

When Czechoslovakia became a dual federation in 1968, the Czech Parliament (the "Czech National

*Up and down these noble flights
of stairs within Thun Palace
have passed the members of Bohemia's
representative government for
over two hundred years.
Traditionally it was the Diet
that sat in this grand residence – a Baroque mansion
radically rebuilt in 1801 following
a disastrous fire – but since 1993
the governing body has been known
as the Parliament of the Czech Republic.*

Council") chose to take up residence in Thun Palace, but only in the last decade has the huge old mansion been modernized for this purpose. In January 1993 the National Council evolved into the Parliament of the Czech Republic. With Thun Palace as its seat, the governing body establishes historical continuity with the ancient democratic traditions of the Bohemian Estates and bourgeoisie.

203

Rohan Palace

This rare gem of Neoclassical architecture, situated in Prague's Karmelitská Street, was built in 1792 by Joseph Zobel for Count Jan Adalbert Czernín von Chudenitz. In 1799, after Count Czernín sold the palace to Princess Paula von Hohenzollern-Hechingen, daughter of Duke Peter of Kurland, the new owner had the Vienna-based Belgian architect Louis Montoyer redesign the interior in its present form. The ballroom and bedchamber have long been regarded as the most outstanding examples of the French Empire style in Prague.

In 1816 Count Victor de Rohan, from one of the premier families of the old French *noblesse,* acquired the property. Steadfastly loyal to the Bourbon monarchy, even after the execution of Louis XVI in 1793, the Rohans fought against the revolutionary Republic of France by joining the Austrian Army. (Marie-Antoinette, the unfortunate Queen of France, was the daughter of Empress Maria Theresia and the sister of Emperor Joseph II, thus an Archduchess of Austria at time of her marriage to the Dauphin, the future Louis XVI.) Eventually, the Rohans gave up the struggle in favor of settling in Bohemia, where they acquired the Inkolat and many estates in the country.

The present façade, with its monumental Corinthian pilasters, was built in the Empire style by

Vinzenz Kulhánek at the behest of Prince Camille de Rohan.

above: *An exquisite Neo-Rococo heating stove set within a niche on the white and gold interior of Rohan Palace.*

above right: *The grand staircase with its elegantly severe wrought-iron balustrade styled in the Empire manner.*

The main façade of
Rohan Palace with
itz series of giant
Corinthian pilasters
marching across
the central pavilion.

Schebeck Palace

Although 19th-century Prague, with its hilly terrain, could not have an extended modern thoroughfare such as Vienna's Ringstrasse, erected in the 1860s on the cleared site of the old "ring" of defensive walls, the city boasted, as it does today, several concentrations of imposing palaces, whether houses, banks, or mercantile establishments. One such area stands on the border between Old and New Towns near the former municipal park facing Franz Joseph Station (now known as the Main or Wilson Station). This is the "Lower New Town," where, unfortunately, the great houses have not always been well maintained. An important exception is the dignified exterior of Schebeck Palace in Politickych veznu. It came into being when Jan Schebeck, a rail and real-estate baron who had become one of Bohemia's first self-made technocrats, commissioned Ignác Ullmann to erect an ostentatious mansion on the site of a former orphanage. Ullmann, the leading architect in contemporary Prague, seized on the occasion to fashion a façade that would depart somewhat from the horizontality he normally favored. The new vertical emphasis falls mainly on the entrance portico, a triumphal arch ensemble composed of a

above and left: *The street façade of Schebeck Palace with its monumental entrance portal styled like a triumphal arch.*

opposite: *The grand staircase is decorated with a program of frescoes in which Victor Barvitius combined the Olympian gods with personifications of the arts, zodical signs, and* grottesche.

206

Coffered ceilings in
Schebeck Palace. In the ballroom,
Victor Barvitius painted episodes from
the lives of Johann Schebeck's ancestors.

tall, round-headed central opening flanked by niches with allegorical statues by Joseph Wagner and pairs of colossal, freestanding Corinthian columns. These support a shallow balcony whose balustrade is continuous with that of the pedimented windows on

the piano nobile. Heavily rusticated below and ashlar smooth above, the grandiose Schebeck façade looks onto a wide street leading to the onetime New German Theater, now the State Opera House.

The scenes painted in the lunettes
of the ballroom's upper walls chronicle
key episodes in the mythical past of
the Schebeck family. The paintings would
have us believe taht the grandmother of
Johann Schebeck, one of 19th-century
Bohemia's first self-made technocrats,
was tending sheep when an eagle swooped
down upon the grazing flock, only to be
driven away by a handsome young hunter.
After falling in love, the shepherdess and
her savior married and founded a dynasty.

209

Villa Lanna

Something fresh appeared in Prague architecture during the 1860s – suburban villas erected for the new elite composed mainly of bankers and building contractors in search of a second residence. One of the loveliest examples is the asymmetrical Neo-Renaissance villa that Anton Barvitius and Ignác Ullmann erected on a slope above the former village square in what is now Prague's Bubeneč district. This was once a picturesque village, which became a small town in 1904 before its incorporation into the city of Prague in 1920. Dominating the façade of the monumentally simple, blocky structure is a two-story portico supported by paired Tuscan pilasters below and Ionic square and cylindrical columns above. Of the two architects, Barvitius may have been the more active, especially in Rome during the years 1856–66, when he converted Palazzo Venezia into a residence for the Austrian Ambassador.

Adalbert Lanna the Younger, for whom Barvitius and Ullmann erected the villa, had not only inherited the talents of his father, a shipbuilder and contractor from Budweis who gave Prague its first suspension bridge and first stone quay; he also emerged as the greatest patron of the arts and the most enthusiastic collector in the Bohemian capital during the second half of the 19th century. After commissioning Viktor Barvitius, the architects

brother, to decorate the interior of the villa, the owner hung it with works by Hans Makart and the contemporary German masters Adolph Menzel and Leopold Rottmann. Today the well-preserved Villa Lanna houses the Academy of Sciences.

above: The elegant dining room in Villa Lanna boasts an elaborate Neoclassical décor by Viktor Barvitius.

opposite: The highly Classicized Villa Lanna is fronted by a two-story entrance portico and backed by a tower culminating in a loggia and a balustraded attic.

Villa Groebe

In 1871, 19th-century Prague gained its most magnificent villa when Moritz August Groebe, building contractor and associate of Adalbert Lanna and Jan Schebeck, commissioned Anton Barvitius to erect a suburban residence beyond the city walls on the edge of Wimmer Park. The very embodiment of what local taste regarded as the perfect Italian villa, the Groebe mansion stands on the sun-drenched southern slope of the Nusle Valley. It is in fact a three-story Renaissance palace, with an interior decorated in the Pompeian style by Josef Schulz and a loggia opening onto ample, beautifully landscaped gardens spread over terrain where plantations and vineyards once flourished. Sparing no expense, Groebe had some 60,000 truckloads of earth brought in from the building site of the Franz Joseph Railway Station. The new gardens featured terraces, artificial grottoes, flights of steps, a fountain with a statue of Neptune by Bohuslav Schnirch, and even some of the old vineyards.

Before the gardens could be completed, modern blocks of flats began to rise nearby, thus creating a satellite suburb typical of the kind of settlement that grew up around Prague in the second half of the 19th century. Following the death of Moritz Groebe, a society of vintners bought the garden around the villa and turned it into a municipal park. Towards the end of World War II a bomb fell on Villa Groebe, destroying the interior and all its furnishings. The building itself would be transformed into a youth hostel in 1953.

above: *The north façade and its ground-floor loggia.*

opposite: *The grand staircase with its coffered, Renaissance ceiling and its walls decorated in the Neo-Pompeian style, complete with grottesche.*

PRAGUE
The
Golden
City

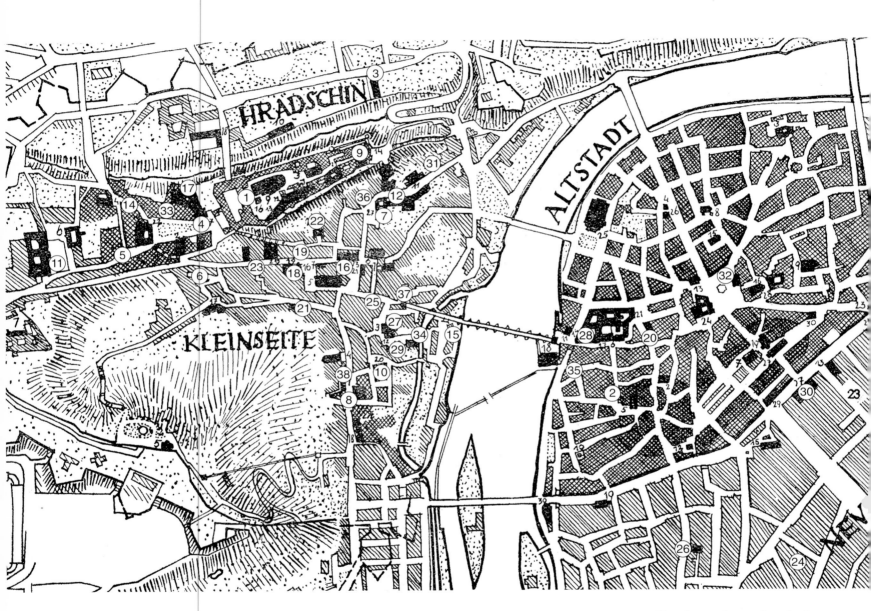

For a key to the numbered palaces and their locations on this map, see the Contents on page 5.

216